GROWING NATIVE HAWAIIAN PLANTS

A How-to Guide for the Gardener

REVISED EDITION

HEIDI LEIANUENUE BORNHORST

BESS PRESS

3565 Harding Avenue
Honolulu, Hawai'i 96816
phone: (808) 734-7159
fax: (808) 732-3627
e-mail: sales@besspress.com
http://www.besspress.com

Illustrations: Karen Bento
Design: Carol Colbath
Photographs: Heidi Leianuenue Bornhorst (unless otherwise indicated)

Library of Congress Cataloging-in-Publication Data

Bornhorst, Heidi Leianuenue.
    Growing native Hawaiian plants : a how-to guide
for the gardener / Heidi Leianuenue Bornhorst. —
Rev. ed.
        p. cm.
    Includes illustrations
    ISBN 1-57306-207-3
    1. Gardening – Hawaii. 2. Gardens – Hawaii.
3. Plants – Hawaii. 4. Tropical plants.
I. Title
SB453.2H3.B67 2005   635.9'069–dc20

Copyright 2005 by Bess Press, Inc.

Printed by Sun Fung Offset Binding Co., Ltd., in China

CONTENTS

BASIC PROPAGATION ADVICE XIV

GROUND COVERS 18

GRASSES AND SEDGES **30**

SHRUBS **35**

DEDICATION

To all gardeners, especially those who marvel over the gift of our native Hawaiian plants and have the courage and conviction to grow and nurture them.

ACKNOWLEDGMENTS

Many people have been vital to me in my horticultural career over the years. My husband, Clark, has helped and encouraged our gardens and me. Dave Boynton sparked my interest in native Hawaiian plants in early high school. Jenny Brady, Dr. Richard Criley, Dave Hollway, Dr. Diane Ragone, Paul Weissich, and Masa Yamauchi were excellent bosses. Botanical *kupuna* "Tūtū" May Moir is a mentor for flower arranging, landscaping, and life. Aunty Beatrice Krauss inspired me with her knowledge of ethnobotany and basic plant science. Both of these women inspired me to write, from a young age. Winona Char, my botanical "big sister," encouraged me to take difficult botany and taxonomy classes. My wonderful family, Karl, Marilyn, and Mimi Bornhorst, and Clark Leavitt supported me through various aspects of my career and education. My surfing buddy and fellow graduate student Lynne Kaneshiro made me get wet once in a while and helped me keep it all in perspective.

Premiere plant propagators Bill Garnett, Baron Horiuchi, Liz Hupman, Kevin Kojima, Kerin Lileeng-Rosenberger, Jeanine Lum, Ronald Matsuda, Randy Mew, Dave Miranda, Rachel Morton, Richard Nakagawa, Jonel Smith, Nellie Sugii and Hideo Teshima shared their experiences and techniques. Excellent field botanists and horticulturists like Carol Ah Toong, Jennifer Higashino, Tim Flynn, Lorrin Gill, Bob Hobdy, "Uncle" Sol Kaopuiki, Joel Lau, David Lorence, Art Medeiros, John Obata, Jimmy Pang, Steve Perlman, and Deborah Ward let me hike along, "talk plants," and learn from them.

In short, I thank all people who are interested in native Hawaiian plants. You have inspired me over the years, and I feel that things are getting better for native Hawaiian plants both in the wild and in cultivation, thanks to all the well-directed efforts of many people like you. *Mahalo nui loa.*

NATIVE HAWAIIAN PLANTS IN THE URBAN LANDSCAPE

In 2003, forestry in Hawai'i celebrated one hundred years of growth and protection. While forestry in Hawai'i is well ahead of forestry in the nation as a whole, until recently, mostly nonnative trees were grown, often because they are easier to grow and tougher than natives. Now forestry is reversing the trend and growing more native Hawaiian trees and fostering entire native ecosystems.

When my siblings and I were growing up here, my parents exposed us to the joys and beauty of the forests of Hawai'i, and to all the nature around us. I remember hiking up Tantalus as my mother told us the *mo'olelo* about how all the birds were invisible (and they were to us, hidden by dense layers of overhanging trees and plants) until that *kolohe* god Māui made them visible.

We played a family car game that involved observing favorite plants and trees and natural features along the way. We'd watch for the strangler fig Chinese banyan (*Ficus retusa*) and see the progress it made enveloping a coconut, just *mauka* of Queen Emma Summer Palace. When I was about thirteen, the banyan finally won. We could see no trace of the poor coconut below layers of enveloping *Ficus*. My mom made us look for all the waterfalls going up Nu'uanu. "Any of you kids see the upside down waterfall yet?" Today we can't see any of those waterfalls; they are obscured by overly successful "panic plantings" of alien weed trees.

When I drive up the *pali* I get out my visual chain saw and remove all the tall, weedy trees, to open up and expand my childhood views and leave only the native trees to grow in peace and splendor: *koa*, *māmaki*, *lehua 'āhihi*. They would replace the *Albizia*, *Eucalyptus*, *Ficus*, cinnamon, and others waiting to crack and drop a branch on top of passersby.

My mother had come under the guidance and teaching of master Hawaiian naturalist Lorrin Gill. She told stories of his gently moving a spider's web out of the way of the hiking teachers in the Wai'anae. She shared Gill's teaching with us, and years later my *ku'uipo* Clark and I joined Lorrin on many of his forest adventures on O'ahu and the neighbor islands. We saw and learned so much, and we still pass on some of his extensive knowledge and Hawaiiana lore and *mo'olelo* to fellow hikers and plant lovers.

The ancients lived amidst many native plants, finding them beautiful and useful. Since Western contact, the fascination with exotics (today we call them "aliens") and the search for large-scale economic uses have crowded out and exterminated native Hawaiian plants in the areas where people live and work. As more and more people have become interested in all aspects of Hawaiiana, including native plants vital to the culture—those used in hula and for making lei, *kapa*, dye, medicines, and canoes—native Hawaiian plants, especially those with known uses, are becoming more and more popular and prevalent in Hawai'i gardens. Once thought to be a passing fad, native plants are becoming permanently rooted into our urban landscapes. Many are tough and attractive and are selected for these qualities alone.

My husband and I play a game in which we walk through a neighborhood and try to spot natives. There's an *'ōhi'a lehua*! A *loulu* palm! A Hawaiian *wiliwili*! We are all winning more often in this strolling-for-views-of-natives-in-the-garden game.

BOTANICAL GARDENS

Botanical gardens are a great repository for and source of plant materials. They are scientific collections of plants and data about how and where the plants were collected and grown in the nursery and how they survived and thrived planted in the garden. Knowing the true provenance, or source, of native plants is vital. Finding the best horticultural techniques and then sharing cultivars and information with growers and the public are services of botanical gardens.

We have a wealth of botanical gardens in Hawai'i, in a variety of microclimates. This benefits rare and wonderful native Hawaiian plants, as well as rare and unusual plants from elsewhere in the tropical world.

Advanced and specialized horticultural techniques such as tissue culture are employed at Lyon Arboretum for some threatened and endangered Hawaiian plants. Good nursery techniques and dedicated propagators at various gardens are adding to the perpetuation of natives and our knowledge about growing them successfully.

Hoʻomaluhia Botanical Garden in Kāneʻohe received an urban forestry grant in 2001, from America the Beautiful and Kaulunani. We had grown natives for years but had not had the trained scientific staff to closely monitor and investigate details about the young trees as they grew in a nurturing environment. The grant allowed us to research, design, plant out, and intensely maintain the young trees for the first year of growth. Ten specimens each of ten target tree species that were deemed to have potential for Hawaiian urban landscapes were planted by staff and community volunteers. The ten species tested were

ʻōhiʻa lehua	*Metrosideros polymorpha*
alaheʻe	*Psydrax odoratum*
hōʻawa	*Pittosporum spp.*
mānele	*Sapindus saponaria*
lonomea	*Sapindus oahuensis*
loulu palm	*Pritchardia martii*
ʻoheʻohe	*Tetraplasandra hawaiiensis*
naio	*Myoporum sandwicensis*
ʻaʻaliʻi	*Dodonaea viscosa*
kokiʻo keʻokeʻo	*Hibiscus waimeae*

Pink ʻaʻaliʻi

Educational materials and programs were built around this urban forestry test garden, which is part of the larger landscape of Kahua Lehua, the native Hawaiian plant section of Hoʻomaluhia. We found out many things about soil needs and pH, insects and diseases.

IT TAKES KŌKUA AND COOPERATIVE GROWING EFFORTS

As clients request—in fact, demand—native Hawaiian plants, and landscape architects become familiar with and specify natives; as nursery growers gear up to produce and maintain natives for the landscape trade; and as landscape managers, grounds staff, and home gardeners become familiar with the wide array of choice plants and their maintenance requirements, we will see more successful plantings of natives.

To help you successfully grow a greater variety of native plants, this revised edition of *Growing Native Hawaiian Plants* includes new information about xeriscaping, water gardening, and growing natives as potted plants on your lanai or in the house. It also includes new ground cover plants, shrubs, ferns, and trees, a new section on grasses and sedges, and new photos. Some of the new plants, like *nāʻū, ʻiliahi, and maʻo*, are rare and endangered natives that we haven't been able to grow (either legally or horticulturally) until recently.

Kokiʻo keʻokeʻo, *or* Hibiscus arnottianus var parviflora, *is a two-day flower that is native to the Waiʻanae Mountains. This is a prime variety for growing and perpetuating in Hawaiʻi gardens.*

INTRODUCTION

If you are one of the many people who would like to grow native plants, this book can help you. Native Hawaiian plants have the reputation of being insignificant "weeds" that are impossible to grow. I can show you that this is not true. Native plants are beautiful in both striking and subtle ways, and if you follow basic, commonsense horticulture, with some extra-keen observation of how your plants are growing and a bit

BELOW: *Steep, wet, furrowed places like these rugged ridges mauka of Hoʻomaluhia Botanical Garden offer many varied habitats for native Hawaiian plants. The bold geography, warm ocean, abundant rainfall, and tropical temperatures create microclimates where many different plants can find their niche, grow, thrive, and evolve into unique Hawaiian life forms.*

of extra care and vigilance, you can happily and successfully grow native Hawaiian plants.

NATIVE VS. INTRODUCED

Native Hawaiian plants are those that came to Hawaiʻi on their own—people did not bring them here. Their seeds or pollen reached the Hawaiian Islands by natural means: some were blown here by jet stream air currents or storm winds, some floated in on ocean currents, some hitchhiked on or in birds.

Once these seeds reached the Hawaiian Islands, which happened only rarely, if they managed to survive and reproduce they had reached Paradise. There

were many places they could grow and thrive—from hot, dry windy coasts, air filled with ocean spray, to dryland gulches, wet lowland forests, rain forests, and high cool mountain areas, to name just a few of the different ecological niches.

Much adaptive radiation and speciation has occurred in Hawai'i's native plants over the millions of years since their arrival, aided by the birds and insects that evolved along with the plants. Our largest native Hawaiian fruit, the *'akala*, a thornless raspberry, is about as big as a strawberry. Most Hawaiian fruits are even smaller, about the size of an olive, making a good meal for a bird, which would eat the seed and eventually "plant" it with some bird kukai for fertilizer. Flightless birds, now extinct, may have helped to disperse many native plant seeds. Birds were also the pollinators of many plants; *'ōhi'a lehua* and *wiliwili*, for example, make lots of nectar and thus attract pollinating birds. The myriad insects were also pollinators.

The plants that evolved into species unique to Hawai'i are called **endemic** plants. Some of Hawai'i's endemic plants are *'ōhi'a lehua*, silverswords, *loulu* palms, and *ko'oloa 'ula*. **Indigenous** plants, which are also considered native, are found naturally in Hawai'i and in many other parts of the world as well. Many indigenous plants arrived long ago, but, unlike endemics, never changed. One of the best examples of an indigenous plant that has spread widely is *naupaka kahakai*. The seeds can float in the ocean for years and still germinate when they wash ashore. To remember the difference between endemic and indigenous plants, think of endemic plants as those that ENDed up here and are the END result of their evolution in Hawai'i. Indigenous plants floated IN or were carried IN by birds, and still have the possibility of coming IN.

Introduced, or **alien**, plants were brought to Hawai'i by people, either on purpose or by accident. When the Polynesians first discovered these islands, they brought thirty or so different plant species and four kinds of animal with them in their sailing canoes. Many more plants and animals have been brought by later arrivals. These modern introductions include plants brought on purpose by agriculturalists and horticulturalists, or by accident as seeds on clothing, in nonsterile potting soil, or in the stomachs of pets, to name only a few possibilities. The landscape was and continues to be drastically altered; the main vegeta-

An *'apapane sips nectar and pollinates* 'ōhi'a lehua. *Native Hawaiian birds and insects co-evolved with native plants. They are vital to each other's survival. Photo by Dave Boynton.*

tion we see around us in our daily lives is a "transplanted landscape."

What we call transplanted landscapes make the Islands beautiful, provide flowers to wear in our hair, and give us good things to eat, shade trees, and wood for shelter and carving. But many of the introduced animals and plants, along with their alien diseases, threaten the benevolent native Hawaiian plants.

WHY GROW NATIVE HAWAIIAN PLANTS?

The field of horticulture—which has cultivated and developed many rare, exotic, and "difficult to grow" plants such as orchids, anthuriums, and bromeliads—has largely ignored native Hawaiian plants. Only a few private hobbyists and botanical gardens have brought native Hawaiian plants into cultivation. Consequently, in populated areas, native Hawaiian plants are rarely seen. You need to go to rugged, inaccessible coasts or high in the mountains to see native plants growing naturally.

Fortunately, state, city, and county governments and private growers are beginning to realize that native Hawaiian plants are not only beautiful but beneficial to the environment. They can be successfully grown and mass-produced for public and private landscapes as well as for reforestation of our native forests and vital, life-giving watersheds. Many native plants, especially those native to coastal and dry forest areas, will help reduce wasteful watering practices.

They are ideal for **xeriscaping,** or less-thirsty landscaping. For example, plants such as *naio, 'a'ali'i, pōhinahina, 'ilima, naupaka, mānele* and *lonomea* have broad-range elevational tolerance. Thus, given full sun and good drainage, they can be grown in coastal, inland, and upland Hawaiian gardens. In the cooler, wetter areas, these plants, once established, require minimal water. They are excellent candidates for the xeriscape garden. Growing plants such as these will help Hawai'i's efforts toward water-conserving landscapes.

Perhaps the most important reason to grow native plants is that many are unique to Hawai'i and are becoming endangered in the wild. A number of native plant species in Hawai'i have become rare and threatened or are already extinct. With good, commonsense horticulture, including growing plants commercially from cultivated source material, native Hawaiian plants need not become extinct. An added benefit is that using native plants will make Hawai'i's landscaping distinctive. Our hotels, parks, golf courses, and gardens do not need to be clones of those of other tropical areas.

SELECTING NEW VARIETIES OF NATIVE HAWAIIAN PLANTS

Now that we know some of the basic horticulture and have brought some plants back from the brink of extinction and into garden cultivation, we can learn more and make some varietal selections.

Some of the many Hawaiian plants that lend themselves easily to varietal selection are *naio, 'a'ali'i,* the hibiscuses and their relatives, *'ilima,* and *ko'oloa 'ula.* Our native Gardenia *brighamii* now has many, many more trees and plants in cultivation in Hawai'i gardens than there are trees in the wild. We are already seeing some varieties in the nursery trade, like the *lau nui,* or "big-leafed" form of the *nā'ū,* or native Hawaiian gardenia. There are already some named varieties of hibiscus, like Kanani Kea, Rice White, Hawaiian Wedding, Sadie Seymour, and more.

Plants with a broad natural range, like *'a'ali'i,* or Dodonaea, can be selected for appearance, including seedpod and leaf color, as well as for type of garden habitat.

A curving graveled pathway invites you into the Hawaiian garden at Lyon Arboretum, envisioned and designed by Liz Huppman and implemented by Huppman, Ken Seamon, and many community volunteers, interns, and students from Hawai'i and around the world. On the left is a clump of 'uki'uki and on the right a patch of 'ahu'awa. The golden-headed flowering shrub is ko'oko'olau. Alahe'e, koa, and 'ōhi'a lehua are among the background shrubs. An interpretive graphic sign funded by a grant from Kaulunani beckons the visitor into the educational and inspirational garden. Photo courtesy of Liz Huppman.

A carpet of hinahina *grows on a remote protected area on the windward shores of O'ahu. An* 'akoko *and native* 'aki'aki *grass add to the silvery tapestry of intermingled coastal plants.* Hinahina *is an ideal plant for lei makers to grow in home gardens and community lei gardens, nurtured by the* hālau.

ACQUIRING NATIVE PLANTS

We need to ensure that plants in their wild habitat are protected and perpetuated, not injured or depleted. It is best to acquire plants from either your favorite nursery or from a friend's garden. If you do bring the plants from the wild into garden cultivation, you should collect sparingly from each plant or area. Obtain the proper permits from the landowners and adhere to their conditions. Some plants are on the state or federal Endangered Species lists. Some of these are easy to grow and beautiful for landscaping. The permit process is getting easier and more reasonable, thanks to the efforts of many concerned plant people in communication with the government agencies that make the rules.

A NOTE ON PLANT NAMES AND CLASSIFICATIONS

When it comes to native Hawaiian plant names and classifications, I am a stubborn "red dirt and black sand farmer." For everyday use, I like Hawaiian names. Although these names may vary from island to island, with several names for each plant, they are easy to pronounce and remember.

Scientific names illustrate the history of a plant and its relationships to other plants. As taxonomists make new discoveries, scientific names undergo changes. 'Ōhi'a lehua is a good example. It has many different growth forms, flower colors, and leaf shapes, sizes, and textures. It grows in many habitats, from the wet coasts, to rain forests, to the highest, soggiest bogs. It grows on nearly virgin lava and on ancient forest soils. Most plants outside Hawai'i don't act this way; they grow in only one type of habitat. 'Ōhi'a lehua has had myriad scientific names, as scientists try to describe and categorize all the forms and types of habitats. Most types of 'ōhi'a are now called *Metrosideros polymorpha*. *Polymorpha* means many forms!

The scientific names I use in this book correspond to those listed in the *Manual of the Flowering Plants of Hawai'i*, by Warren L. Wagner, Derral R. Herbst, and S. H. Sohmer. However, many of the common family names I use are those most recognizable to local gardeners (for example, the hibiscus and lychee families). My main objective is to get people to know and grow our wonderful native Hawaiian plants. After all, an 'ōhi'a lehua by any other name would be just as precious to us.

My favorite Hawaiian plant book is Marie Neal's *In Gardens of Hawai'i*. In includes interesting facts, legends, and ethnobotany and covers most of our native plants. The only thing missing is how to grow and care for the plants and use them in our own gardens.

Kathy Valier's *Ferns of Hawai'i* is my source for fern names, both scientific and Hawaiian. Kathy also graciously let me use her information on ferns and Hawaiian culture.

BASIC PROPAGATION ADVICE

GROWING PLANTS FROM CUTTINGS

Many people like to pinch a piece of a new, exciting, or desirable plant and grow it. Some people like to stick the cutting (slip) in a glass of water on a sunny window sill, wait for it to root, and then plant it in a pot or in the ground. This method is okay for plants that are easy to root, like common hibiscus or ti. But for other plants this does not work so well. Plants put out a different type of root in water than they do in soil, so plants started in water will have to send out new roots in the soil. Some plants do not like all that water in their root zone, and these will rot or just never send out roots.

The best way to grow a plant from cuttings is as follows:

Cut a small twig (2–4 inches long, or with two or three nodes) off the parent plant with a sharp, clean pair of clippers. If you are away from home, pack the cutting in moist sphagnum moss or in moist paper towels in a plastic bag. Keep the cuttings in a cool place away from sun and get home and propagate them as soon as possible. (A small cooler with your chilled lunch and a frozen can of juice or a water bottle works really well to keep both your new cuttings and you cool and hydrated.) If you are making the cutting from a plant in your own garden, better yet, because time is of the essence in getting your cutting started. When you get home (or right away in your garden), recut the lower end (just a snip to expose fresh tissue for rooting), dust it in rooting hormone if you like, and stick the cutting in a pot of growing medium.

My favorite medium for starting cuttings is a mixture of perlite and vermiculite. The vermiculite, which holds too much moisture for a permanent potting mixture, is great for holding moisture to get the new plant started. You can place the cutting in its own small pot, or you can stick several cuttings in a larger pot. Start the cutting in a shady area and gradually move it into a sunnier place. Water as often as you can. Watering several times a day is good. A cutting has no roots of its own, yet the leaves are still giving off moisture; this is why we cut off all the lower leaves and cut the upper leaves in half—to keep the cutting from drying out as the leaves give off moisture. Leave the newest leaves at the tip of the cutting on. These have lots of hormones that chemically signal the cutting to form roots.

Commercial growers use a mist system to keep a film of water on the leaves and to prevent moisture loss. Home growers can use other techniques or can invest in a mist system if they want to grow lots of cuttings of rare Hawaiian plants.

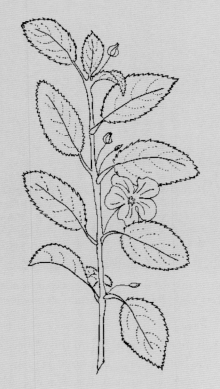

Collect a vigorous, healthy cutting, preferably one that is growing upward into the full sun. Try to get one without fruit, flowers, or buds, as these take away energy needed for the cutting to root.

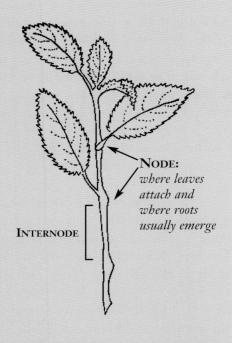

NODE: *where leaves attach and where roots usually emerge*

INTERNODE

Cut off the lower leaves for best rooting. Cut off fruits, flowers and buds, and excess leaves; cut upper leaves in half to conserve moisture.

If the planted cutting retains its leaves, this is a good sign that it is forming new roots. You should still gently check to see if roots are forming. You can dig down carefully and look for roots, or you can wait until new roots emerge from the pukas at the bottom of the pot. Some plants will send out new shoots and retain their leaves but produce no roots. This is where a rooting hormone like Rootone or Hormex, applied when you make the cutting, helps. Rooting hormones send a chemical message to the plant, encouraging it to form roots.

When the plant has formed roots, transplant it into a mixture of peat moss, perlite, and perhaps a little soil from the place where you will put it in the ground. Get rid of as much of the vermiculite as you can without breaking or damaging roots. I like to use a transplanting vitamin solution like Upstart or Superthrive, especially if I am working with a rare or precious plant, or if a lot of roots have been broken during transplanting. I put this solution in a watering can and pour it over the potting mix of the newly transplanted cutting.

Move the transplanted cutting back to where you were propagating it, and then gradually move it to its permanent location in your garden.

GROWING PLANTS FROM SEEDS

Growing plants from seeds is a rewarding experience. The miracle of a tiny seed turning first into a plant and ultimately a tree, bush, or vine is amazing. Plants grown from seed will have a healthy, strongly branched, and natural root system. If you want to grow native Hawaiian or other rare and endangered plants, collecting and growing seeds causes the least impact on the plant and its ecosystem.

Seeds and young seedlings can be thought of as young human infants and treated with the same care. The more healthy, sanitary, and nutritious start in life you can give them, the more healthy and vigorous they will be as adults.

To start seeds, use a sterile potting mix. I like to use fine peat moss and perlite. Put a 50:50 mix in a clean 6-inch pot. Wet the medium thoroughly and pack it down firmly with the bottom of another clean pot.

An important consideration is how deep to plant the seeds. A good rule of thumb (this makes for a "greener thumb"!) is to plant the seeds as deep as the diameter of the seed. For example, a tiny seed of *ʻōhiʻa lehua* would be sown right on the surface of the wet, firm potting medium, then lightly dusted with a very fine potting medium. A bigger seed, like that of *wiliwili*, would be covered by 1/4 to 1/2 inch of medium. After carefully planting the seeds (several to a 6-inch pot), water thoroughly, firm gently with another pot bottom, and put the pot of seeds on a bench. In Hawaiʻi it is best to keep the pots off the ground. Bufos like to sit in moist media, and slugs may attack the young seedlings. Water daily.

When the seeds have germinated (sprouted), wait until the

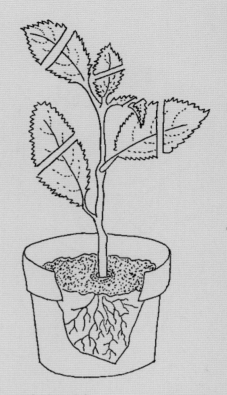

Remove buds and flowers so energy is used to grow roots, cut leaves in half to conserve water, and put rooted cuttings in the right size pot: not too huge, but with space to allow for root growth.

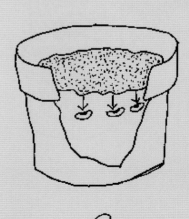

Cover as deep as the width of the seeds.

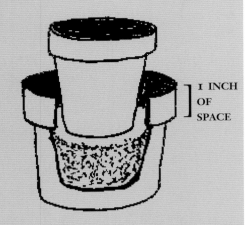

] I INCH
OF
SPACE

Firm soil with another clean pot. Leave about 1 inch of space between the top of the planting medium and the lip of the pot to allow for thorough watering.

Pot up seedlings as rooted cuttings in pots that are the right size to accommodate the roots (not too big or they'll "drown"– not too small or the roots will dry out and start to spiral in the pot).

young seedlings have two sets of leaves (or look big and strong enough to survive transplanting). Transplant the seedlings into individual pots that are deep enough to accommodate their roots without bending them. Put a pinch of fertilizer in the bottom third of the pot with the same kind of mixture you used for the seeds. Carefully place the seedlings in their individual pots and fill in the mixture around their roots. Be very careful to plant the seedlings as deep as they were in the original seed pot. If you are unsure, look at the stem, roots, and potting mix to determine the proper depth. If the seedlings are planted too deep they may rot, and if too shallow the roots will dry out. Either condition could kill the seedling.

I like to set up a "mini factory" when I set out to transplant my seedlings or cuttings. I get the planting medium all mixed and select several pot sizes that I think will accommodate the seedlings or rooted cuttings. Some of the new plants will have larger root systems than others and will need bigger, deeper pots; some will be smaller and need to go in smaller, shallower pots. I put some medium in the bottom third of the pots, mix in some organic or slow-release fertilizer, and then gently pull the original pot off and hold the seedlings and medium in my hand. (We call the pot with lots of seedlings or cuttings a "community pot.") If there are lots of seedlings or cuttings, lay out some moist paper towels or newspapers to wrap around the seedlings that still need to be separated out, to keep them moist. Gently pull the roots of the seedlings apart. Stick the seedlings in their own pots and add medium around their roots. The seedling should go in the center of the pot so its roots can spread out evenly in all directions. The top of the medium should be 1/2 to 1 inch below the rim of the pot. This allows plenty of water to flow into the pot and keep the keiki moist when you water. Again, keep the seedlings at the same level in the pot and gently firm the medium around the roots with your fingers. Have a watering can or pitcher of water nearby. Water the plant thoroughly as soon after transplanting as possible. This is why a filled watering can is a good thing to have on hand. You can water as soon as you repot each plant. A commercially available vitamin B1 transplanting solution can help to lessen transplant shock. I always use this when transplanting rare plants, or if many roots were broken during transplanting.

Keep the plant in the same type of environment as it was before—for example, sun or shade. If many roots are broken, trim off some of the leaves to compensate for the loss of roots. After potting a batch, soak them well with the watering can, firm again with your fingers, and adjust the amount of potting medium.

When the seedlings are big and tough enough, you can plant them in the ground or transplant them to a larger pot. When planting in the ground, mix in compost or cinders to improve the soil and its drainage—few plants survive in standing water. Add some fertilizer in the bottom of the hole and mix it into the bottom half of the soil/compost/cinder mix; you want to fertilize the roots of your plant, not the surrounding weeds or lawn. Water well after planting and then daily until the plant is well established.

Growing Native Hawaiian Plants

AIR-LAYERING

Air-layering is a horticultural technique based on what plants sometimes do in nature. It is a way to produce new, fairly large plants from another prized plant. Plants that are commonly air-layered include lychee, jabong, hibiscus, and *pua kenikeni*. Native Hawaiian plants that can be air-layered include native hibiscus and *ʻōhiʻa lehua*, and air-layering will probably work for other plants that may not set seed or are difficult to grow from cuttings.

The tools and supplies that you need for air-layering are a sharp, clean knife, sharp, clean clippers, rooting hormone, moist sphagnum moss, strong plastic-wrap pieces about 8 x 12 inches, and wire or string for tying. Select a healthy-looking branch that is growing upward; these usually have the best concentrations of root-promoting hormones. Look for a place in the branch 1 to 2 feet below the tip of the branch that has no side shoots and few leaves. If you can't find such a place on the branch, look for the closest thing, and cut off the side shoots and leaves for about 8 inches with the clippers. With your knife make two slices, about an inch apart, ringing the bark. Between these two slices hold the knife flat against the bark and begin to scrape it carefully. Under the bark you will find a green, slippery layer—the **vascular cambium**. This is where growth and cell division occur. It is also where sugars are transported from the leaves, and minerals and water from the roots. You want to interrupt this transport and get the plant to form roots at the scraped inch of bark. Continue to scrape carefully and remove the thin green layer, all the way around the branch, down to the whitish wood below. When you are down to this wood, apply rooting hormone all over the scraped area, wrap a handful of moist moss around the entire area, and then wrap this in plastic, tying and securing it at both ends. It should look like a small sausage around the branch. The end of the plastic wrap should be on the bottom or lower side of the branch so that irrigation or rain doesn't get in and oversaturate the moss. (Some people use tinfoil, but I find that it dries out too much. Also, birds are attracted to the shiny foil and might tear apart your air-layer). Keep an eye on the air-layer, ensuring that it remains moist. In a month or so, roots will appear, growing in the moss. When the moss is fairly packed with roots, carefully cut off the branch and pot it up in a pot that is about five times greater in volume than the new root mass. Keep the potted branch in a fairly shady area and water it a lot to get the new plant growing successfully on its own new roots. You may want to cut some leaves in half to help retain moisture for the new plant.

Sometimes, as with all gardening techniques, air-layering doesn't work; the branch dies or the air-layered piece just doesn't form roots. There are several reasons for this. The plant might not be a good candidate for air-layering. It could have been a bad time of year to air-layer. Your technique may have been bad: the cut was too deep or not deep and thorough enough, the moss too wet or too dry, and so forth. Don't give up. Try again and write down whatever happens. Keep track of dates and record what worked and what didn't. If the branch didn't die, but also didn't form roots after three or four

AIR-LAYERING SUPPLIES

Clean sharp knife
Clean sharp clippers
Rooting hormone
Moist sphagnum moss
Strong plastic swatches (8 x 12 inches)
Wire or string

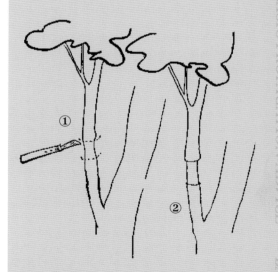

① *Carefully slice two rings in the bark about 1 inch apart.*

② *Carefully remove bark between the two rings.*

③ *Apply rooting hormone all over cut area.*

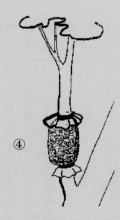

④ *Wrap moist sphagnum moss around cut area, wrap with plastic swatch, tie at top and bottom.*

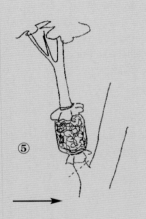

⑤ *Cut rooted air-layer off where shown.*

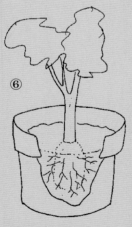

⑥ *Pot rooted air-layer in the right size pot. Water at least daily.*

months, take it apart and check out what happened. You might be able to recut the stem and make it work. Keep trying—that's the fun and challenge of horticulture in Hawai'i!

Note: Sometimes we are overly ambitious in wanting to get a new, big plant right away. Be patient and start with a small branch. You will have better success getting the plant to root, and if your technique is bad, or if the plant is a poor rooter via air-layering, you won't lose a whole big branch of the parent tree.

Another technique, again a mimic of what can happen in the wild, is ground-layering. Bend a supple stem down, cover it with soil or a rock, and new roots will form where the plant is buried. This works well with ground covers such as *pā'ū-o-Hi'iaka*, *'ilima papa*, and *nehe*. With such plants you can train the wild tendrils into newly rooted soil-holding, erosion-preventing parts of the parent plant. Place the tendrils where you need the plant to be fuller. Cover the stem and it will send out roots at that point. You can also cut the tendrils off to make new plants. This is fun and easy, great for teaching gardening to keiki, and definitely "low tech."

GRAFTING

Grafting is a horticultural technique that seems something like magic. You put two pieces from different plants together and get a new, more vigorous plant of a superior variety.

Many plants are commonly grafted: citrus, avocado, macadamia, mango, and hybrid and rare hibiscus. Some may need to be grafted as a technique to save an individual plant or even an entire rare species. The technique is sometimes an emergency, last-ditch measure to keep a plant alive or help it thrive. The rare native *Kokia cookei* (a tree relative of hibiscus with a strikingly different red flower, originally native to Moloka'i) was grafted by horticulturists at Waimea Arboretum after the only wild individual was killed in a fire and none of the seeds from cultivated plants would germinate.

Grafting is a way to get bigger plants and more of them from one or a few individuals. For example, *Hibiscus waimeae* subsp. *hannerae*, native to the wet windward valleys of Kaua'i, was thought to be extinct. It had last been seen in the 1920s in Wainiha Valley, in an area that was now completely overgrown with alien thorny plants. In 1977, Chipper Wichman and Steve Perlman found some plants of this extremely rare Hawaiian hibiscus at the base of a waterfall in a remote valley in the Limahuli Preserve on Kaua'i. We took a specimen to Dr. Harold St. John at the Bishop Museum and verified its identity. We were all ecstatic to find that this wonderful miniature white hibiscus, with its dark pink staminal column and light fragrance, still exists in Hawai'i. A few plants were grown from seeds, but they suffered a root rot on their own roots. Before they completely wilted and died, pieces were successfully grafted onto a rootstock of the pink waterfall hibiscus (which is itself half-Hawaiian) and now grow prolifically.

Grafting takes a lot of skill and practice to perfect, as well as a specially designed, sharp knife. You grow a **stock plant** that has strong, disease-resistant roots. You then cut a **scion** piece of the plant you want to grow. These two pieces are joined together, using one of several types of cutting and placement. For a top wedge, one of the easiest methods, you cut the base of the scion into a wedge. The top of the stock plant gets a flat cut through the stem and is sliced down the middle. The scion is then wedged into the slice. The two are carefully lined up so that the vascular cambium of each (the "veins" just under the bark) matches, and then they are tied and wrapped together and waxed at all open, wounded points. The side wedge method is similar. The scion is again cut into a wedge and inserted into a slice in the side of the stem. With the side wedge, the stock plant keeps its branch and leaves above the graft union. Some people say that this helps the scion "learn" how to grow; others believe that the stock top growth drains away strength for the scion, which is trying to grow.

Budding, a technique similar to grafting, requires an even smaller piece of the variety to be grafted. A vegetative bud and a bit of bark are sliced off, and these are inserted under the bark of the stock plant. This is a more difficult technique to master, but it is well worth the effort to learn this "miracle of horticulture," especially as a way to grow and perpetuate wonderful and rare plants.

WATERING

The amount and timing of water for established plants depend on where you live and what your climate and soil are like. Red clay soils hold more water for a longer period of time than do sandy soils. If your area is very sunny, windy, or near the beach, things will dry out faster. Because we have so many varied types of climate in Hawaiʻi, there is no hard-and-fast rule for watering. Even in one garden there are parts that will need more or less water; soils can vary, and amount of shade and wind are also different. It takes common sense and observation of your plants to water appropriately. After plants are established (a month or two for most plants, or up to a year for some trees), you can start to back off on watering. Try every other day or two and watch your plants for wilting. Water before they get too wilted, or they might die. Keep watching and adjusting your watering schedule to find out what is best for you and your plants.

The less watering we can get away with, the better. Our plants will be tougher, and we will have time to do other things in the garden or in life. Deep, thorough, less-frequent watering is better than frequent shallow watering. Deep watering penetrates to the root level and allows some water to be held in the soil for later use by the plant. Deep watering encourages the plants to grow deeper roots and thus to be less subject to drought, or to times when we cannot water.

For me, watering is a fun and relaxing part of gardening. It gets the day off to a good start and relieves stress at day's end. It is a time to look at my plants, make plans for what to do next in the garden, or just enjoy the zen of the falling droplets. Think of a gentle tradewind rain when you water. Do not blast your plants as if you were putting out a fire; you will wash precious soil away from the roots, or even out of the pot. Droplets that hit the soil too hard can make it compact like cement, and the roots will have a hard time

GROUND-LAYERING
Take a healthy tendril of the desired plant, bend it down, and cover it with soil or weight it down with a rock. When roots have formed, carefully dig them out, cut off the new plant from the mother plant, pot it up, and nurture it to get it growing on its own roots.

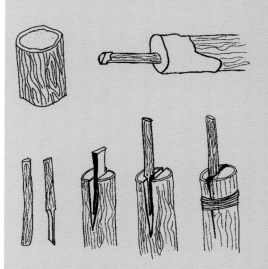

GRAFTING TECHNIQUE
The scion is the piece from the desired plant. The stock is what you graft it onto. Insert the scion into the stock and match up the cambia (green layer under the bark) of the two plants. Tie the scion in place with raffia or stretchy green plant ties, and wax all cut and exposed surfaces. (This is called the top-wedge graft technique.)

penetrating the soil and getting enough oxygen (roots need oxygen too—that's why we till the soil and add soil conditioners like cinder or compost).

There are all kinds of watering nozzles and watering cans that you can buy to help you water properly. I have tried many, but my favorite is my thumb or finger over the hose end. I can control the water, making it come out in a mist or as gentle droplets. I also like to feel that cooling precious Hawaiian water as it flows out of the hose.

Automatic sprinkler systems are nice, especially if you work or travel a lot. But they can be expensive to install, and they must be checked and adjusted regularly. Like any mechanical thing, they can fail or malfunction, and before you notice it, some of your plants are dead.

At Honolulu Botanical Gardens, with its foresightful director Paul Weissich, and at the Board of Water Supply's Hālawa Xeriscape Garden, I worked long and hard to grow less-thirsty plants and to develop Hawai'i-specific water-saving methods for Hawaiian gardens. Research in other dry areas of the world with mandatory water restrictions points out one thing: **the most efficient tool for saving water and making sure it gets to the right place is a smart, observant person like you at the end of the hose.**

XERISCAPING WITH NATIVES

The word "xeriscaping" adapts the familiar word "landscaping" with the Greek *xeros*, which means dry. I have coined a new phrase for Hawai'i: "*akamai wai* gardening"—smart water gardening. Paul Weissich conceived and developed a Hawaiian style of water-saving gardening for the Honolulu Botanical Gardens, and home gardeners can practice smart water gardening, too. The plants don't have to be cactus and rocks, or even "zero-scaping" as in places like California, Nevada or Arizona. We have fabulous plants already here, the native plants of dry coastal and forest areas. For millions of years they have been getting by during times with very little water—the long hot summers and other periodic dry times.

Xeriscaping is not yet mandatory in Hawai'i as it is in parts of the mainland. We can prepare for a time when it might become mandatory by cultivating our water-saving native plants now.

The native plants of Hawai'i are excellent for use in xeriscapes or less thirsty gardens. After all, they did evolve here for millions of years through both drought and wet times.

Drought-resistant and less thirsty plants and plants that thrive in windy and salty conditions grow naturally in coastal and dryland forests. However, plants that grow in rain forests and at high elevations may also do well in "*akamai wai*," or water-sensible gardens. For example, *Artemesia mauiensis* from high-elevation, harsh Haleakalā does well in a coastal garden at Lanikai. I guess the plants didn't read the book!

I learned so much about our treasured dryland Hawaiian forests by working intensively in them at Kānepu'u, on Lāna'i, and Honouliuli, on O'ahu. "Dryland forest" is really a misnomer. These

Growing Native Hawaiian Plants

forests are (or were) much wetter than we think. The plants and trees shelter one another and keep the wind at bay and the soil moist and rich from fallen leaves.

Stepping into and under (definitely a short-girl's forest!) the native tree canopy at Kānepu'u was like entering a different world. We tried to imagine this place before the hand of humankind landed so heavily upon it. The howling, soil-blasting wind was stilled under the gnarled trees, the soil was rich and moist, and the diversity of trees was astounding.

Some experts say that the dryland forests of Hawai'i were much more diverse than the rain forests. They have been more heavily hammered because they are near the places where people want to live and work and where the chompers and stompers (introduced grazing hoofed animals) have run amok over the years.

Certain principles unify xeriscape gardening, and we are in the process of adapting these for Hawai'i conditions and landscape design techniques.

Plant palette. Find plants that come from dry, harsh locations. In Hawai'i we have fabulous native plants to choose from. Some have never been cultivated in gardens before. They have not been tested in a variety of microhabitats, soil conditions, and landscape-maintained regimes. We need to test and keep records and keep on growing natives in rigorous conditions to find out what extremes of drought, wind, and salt they can tolerate and still stay alive and look attractive in our gardens.

Many of the Polynesian-introduced plants and trees are good for coastal dry and salty gardens. *Kou milo* and *hala* are very tough and very handsome. They are all less thirsty trees. *Kou* and *hala* are now known to be native to Hawai'i. They were also carried here on the great voyaging canoes of the ancient Hawaiians.

We also have less thirsty nonnative plants that have been in Hawai'i a long time, like plumeria, bougainvillea, royal poinciana, and so on. These mix well and attractively with natives in our "hapa-Hawaiian landscapes."

Botanical gardens, nurseries, and plant enthusiasts have been bringing in new plants from the world tropics to grow in our gardens. With the threat of running out of potable water hanging over our heads for many years now, these professionals have long had an eye out for good-looking, less thirsty plants. These new introductions may also mix well in good landscape designs using natives and introduced plants. As my long-time boss and mentor Paul Weissich has stated, "Hawaiian xeriscapes don't have to be cactus and rocks or "zero–Scapes"; they can and should be attractive and uniquely Hawaiian.

Zone your landscape. Grow plants with similar requirements together. For example, plants that like it hot and dry and thrive in full sun should be planted together in the hottest, driest, SUNNIEST corner of your garden.

Some of us must grow moisture-loving plants like *palapalai* ferns and *'ōhi'a lehua*. Plant them by the hose bib by the entry, where you will water them regularly and often, or plant them in the shadier, moister part of the garden. Plant them together so you can water and add mulch efficiently, and they will help shelter and nurture each other.

Use mulch. Mulch has many benefits. It slows weeds, improves the soil, retains moisture, and can be very attractive. Mulching occurs naturally in the forest, and we can replicate it in our landscapes to our benefit.

Most important, mulch is a protection against poor landscape maintenance techniques and line trimmer debarking. Grow your plants in mulched beds. Make a "mulch dish" around trees and shrubs, especially when they are young. Keep the line trimmers and mowers away from the trunks with correctly placed mulch.

Organic mulch comes in a wide variety in Hawai'i. You can get it from tree trimmers or buy it by the bag or truckload. Softwood trees like *hau* and coconut produce rich mulch that breaks down into life-building compost pretty quickly. Leguminous trees like monkeypods (the leaves are also great for gardening), showers, and weedy acacias produce nitrogen-rich mulch. Hardwood trees like eucalyptus and ironwood produce a longer-lasting slower-to-breakdown mulch. Use this at bed edges to repel weeds.

You can rake up leaves and use them for mulch; lychee leaves are excellent and so are monkeypod and mango. Any leaves work well, and raking tones upper arm flab. No need go gym!

People who have gardened on the mainland or those locals who read mainland organic gardening books will be amazed at how quickly organic mulch breaks down in Hawai'i. The way I developed such nice leg muscles is from the years of climbing sixty stairs with bags of mulch, horse and elephant manure, and raked up monkeypod leaves to nourish the black cinder soil in my parents' yard.

Stone mulch is one great and good-looking technique. We have lots of types of stones to choose from, depending on the soil type, plant requirements, and color scheme of the plant palette. I like red and black cinders a lot. Blue rock is also good looking and long lasting. Coral chips are good for beach plants, but I don't always like the glare of all that white. There are also river rocks and even larger boulders to choose from. Some properties have natural stones that can be sorted out and used for long-lasting, ground-covering, beneficial stone mulch.

There is a proper way to apply mulch. Around trees and shrubs, "make a volcano," says Joanne Pinney of Hanalei. "Make a donut, not a muffin," I tell the city crews. "Make a lei," we say to *keiki* who want to care for trees.

Think of how plants grow in the wild. Think about where their fine feeder roots are. Mulching right up to the trunk is bad and not natural. It can rot the trunk. Keep mulch about 6 inches away from the trunk of trees and at least 3 inches for bushes. Lay it out where the edges of the roots are now, and put some extra to encourage the roots to grow outward from the tree trunk. Envision all those fine root hairs extending out into the soil and harvesting nutrients and moisture trickling down from the mulch.

It seems to save time, but don't make the mulch too thick. About 6 to10 inches deep is good. Reapply every 3 or 4 months.

Check your irrigation. Some gardeners say that the most efficient way to water is to have a smart, observant horticulturist at the end of the hose. Hand watering is relaxing and fun. You also get to check out your plants and wash off any insect pests you might find. Hand watering means you LOOK at every plant and this is the basis of good horticulture—interacting intimately with your plants.

Not everyone can hire me or another professional, so here's some advice about automatic systems. Automatic irrigation systems and drip irrigation systems are fine, but you must check and maintain them. Pro landscapers say to turn on and check the system every week. Imagine the poor golf course superintendent who had a nice automatic irrigation system—absolutely state of the art, computer on desk, weather sensor up the coconut tree. Goes on vacation without a care in the world and one week later all the expensive, perfect, chemical-rich monoculture of turf grass is *make*—die dead.

Observe and plan accordingly. Really look at your garden and assess the conditions. Take your time. A garden is never really *pau*; it is always an evolving work in progress. Plan it well and all will grow well.

What are the wind and sun patterns (throughout the year and at various times of day)? What kind of soil do you have? How close are you to the beach? Do you get salty winds? Where does the soil always dry out first? Where does it stay moist? Does the soil drain well? Good drainage is essential for most plants.

What kinds of plants do you want? How much work do you want to do?

Gardening should be fun. Growing natives should be joyous. Keep records, look at what your neighbors grow, talk to native growers, and don't feel too bad if a plant dies. Try to figure out what went wrong and do it better next time. You can write a book about your gardening experiences too. I hope you do!

As one philosophical gardener told me, "If I try a plant and it doesn't grow well, I move it around in my garden to try and find the right place for it to flourish. Or I try growing something else!"

Limit the amount of grass. Do you have *keiki* who play soccer in the yard? Do you need room to pitch a *pā'ina* tent and dig an *imu*? Do you have a pony? Do you hate to mow, water, fertilize, and apply harsh chemicals for a "perfect golf course lawn"? Consider having less grass. That is one of the xeriscaping principles I (as a maintenance person) love most. As my *hānai tūtū* May Moir would say, "No grass is fine, dear—more room for precious, useful plants." She got rid of all her grass back in the 1930s and put in porous, easy-to-maintain and walk on (no mud in winter) pavers. She retained only a strip of lawn on the outside of her Nu'uanu property.

My botanical buddy Leland Miyano converted his parents' one-acre grass yard into a tropical wonderland with stone-paved paths. Gorgeous—and no mowing!

No turf grass to care for means more time for other fun things: stopping to smell the *koki'o ke'oke'o*, picking *'ōhi'a lehua* for a special lei, and going surfing at sunrise.

TRANSPLANTING

Transplanting seems hard, even scary, to many people. But it is easy once you know how to do it, especially if you set up properly. I like to think of it as a small factory:

1. Use pots that are one size bigger than the potted plant is in.
2. Get potting medium ready.

A good permanent potting medium is a half-and-half mixture of peat moss and perlite. If the plant is from a dry or coastal area, add chunks of cinder or extra perlite. If the plant is from the wet forest, add more peat moss or compost. Be aware that certain plants react severely to acidity, and add peat moss only with the understanding that it is very acidic.

If the plant is eventually to be planted in the ground, make a mix of equal parts peat moss, perlite, and soil. The soil should come from the area where the plant is to be planted. Slow-release fertilizer can be mixed into the potting medium, at rates according to directions on the fertilizer label.

3. Once you have pots, potting medium, fertilizer, and watering can in hand, you are ready to start repotting. The most important rule is to **keep the plant stem at the same depth as it was in the original pot**.

Another important rule is to **avoid putting the plant in too large a pot.** If the pot is too large for the roots of the plant, the plant may not be able to take up all the water in the soil and the roots may "drown" and rot.

Mix your potting medium and add some slow-release fertilizer. Pre-wet the medium to keep the dust down and to lessen the shock to the plant. Put some medium in the bottom of the new pot. Measure for correct depth in the new pot while the plant is still in its old pot. Make sure that there is from 1/2 to 2 inches from the top of the pot so that the plant can get adequate water. Make sure that the stem is the same depth in the medium as it was before. Try to stand the plant upright, and center the stem in the middle of the pot.

Water the plant thoroughly as soon after transplanting as possible. This is why a filled watering can is a good thing to have on hand. You can water as soon as you repot each plant. A commercially available vitamin B1 transplanting solution can help to lessen transplant shock. I always use this when transplanting rare plants, or if many roots were broken during transplanting.

Keep the plant in the same type of environment as it was before, for example, sun or shade. If many roots are broken, trim off some of the leaves to compensate for the loss of roots.

FERTILIZING

There are several methods to get fertilizer to your native Hawaiian plants: foliar fertilizing; incorporation at time of planting or transplanting; puka fertilizing; and broadcasting.

Masa Yamauchi digs carefully to get a good root ball for transplanting donated hāpuʻu from this Wahiawā garden to Wahiawā Botanical Garden.

Growing Native Hawaiian Plants

Foliar fertilizing means applying a liquid fertilizer solution to the leaves and root zone of the plant. There are many tools available for applying fertilizer: pressure sprayer, hose-end siphon, hose-end sprayer, pumping backpack sprayer, even a watering can. I have tested them all and own many of them. The one I prefer is a good old watering can. You can use it easily; it won't clog or malfunction. There are no gaskets or seals to wear out. You can see right where you are putting the fertilizer.

Incorporation is a practical and efficient way to apply fertilizer. You put the fertilizer in the bottom of the planting hole and stir it around if you are placing the plant in the ground. You mix fertilizer into the transplanting medium, especially in the lower third, of a new pot. By incorporating, you are putting the fertilizer right in the area where the plant's roots can reach it best.

Puka fertilizing is another efficient way to get fertilizer right where it is needed. Hawaiian soils tend to "tie up" phosphorous (the middle number of the formula on the fertilizer bag). This means that the phosphorus is tightly held to soil particles by chemical bonds, making it hard for the plant to get this vital nutrient if it is just tossed on the surface of the soil. If you make pukas in the soil and pour the fertilizer down in, the roots can get to it and use it.

To puka fertilize, draw an imaginary line with your eyes from the outer edges of the tree or plant's canopy down to the ground, or look at the shadow the tree casts at noon. This is called the **dripline**. The dripline is where you make the pukas. Use a pick or other sharp-pointed object that will make a hole 3 to 8 inches deep. It is even more efficient to top the fertilizer you pour into the hole with compost. This activates the fertilizer and helps the plant take it up.

Broadcasting fertilizer (tossing or spreading fertilizer on the surface of the soil or planted areas) works well for lawns but does not get the fertilizer down to the roots of trees or shrubs very well. This is what you see commercial gardeners with a big fertilizer budget do sometimes, but it is wasteful and doesn't help your plants as much as the other three methods. If you must broadcast, top the fertilizer with mulch or compost. This serves to keep the nitrogen from escaping into the atmosphere, helps get the phosphorous to the roots, and in general activates the fertilizer.

Fertilizing and pest control tips:

Keep soil properties balanced and harmonious. Use as few chemicals as possible. Feed the soil organics and stones.

Look at your plants, check on them, and watch them grow. Talk to them if you like, sing to them, or scold them into proper growth. Any form of "hot air" from us is a good carbon dioxide source for the plants, so share a little.

As plant scientists say, "Monitor your plants and garden." Look at the leaves and buds for any sign of pests. Often you can just "rub them out"—smash and kill aphids, mealybugs, spit bugs, and other pesky, sap-sucking, new-bud–malforming insects before they really infest your plants.

You can "clean" your plants with biodegradable soaps that smother insects. My favorite is peppermint soap, Dr. Bronners from the health food store. Dilute one tablespoon of soap in one gallon of

DRIPLINE FOR PUKA FERTILIZING
Make pukas in the dripline area (shown by the dotted circular line under the tree canopy).

HEALTHY TREE
This tree has good branch structure, with no weak branch angles, overlapping branches, or dead wood.

water. Spray it onto the infested leaves and the insects themselves. Let the soap sit for an hour or so and then wipe the pests away with a soft cloth or old toothbrush.

Often a black, sooty mold accompanies aphid infestations. Gently wipe the mold off, as it is ugly and blocks photosynthesis.

Chinese rose beetles emerge at dusk and like to feed on many natives like hibiscus, *kokia*, and *ʻōhiʻa lehua*. There are several ways to safely control these rose beetles. You can always "nuke" them with commercial insecticides, but this is not good for YOU or the environment. The pesticides never really kill all of the beetles, and you might be poisoning yourself or those you love. So try to use more environmentally friendly and life-sustaining methods.

UH Extension agent Ed Mersino shared another nonchemical method of staving off rose beetles: erecting a barrier. Dole used 6- or 7-foot-high hoops of wire covered with shade cloth material around many of their orchard trees on the North Shore when the trees were young. The leaves of young mango, lychee, and other fruit trees were being eaten just as young natives are sometimes. The new leaves were being devoured as they started to grow. The shade cloth went all the way to the ground, but the hoops were open on the top. The rationale was that the beetles would fly along at a fairly low elevation and would pass around the hoops. It was an expensive solution, but it seemed to work in an open field. The hoops of black shade cloth weren't the most attractive sights along Kaukonahua Road, but at least they saved the environment from the application of a lot of insecticides. Once the trees were a bit taller, the damage was less and the hoops were removed.

Mike DeMotta, a native grower who lives in the dark hills of Hanapēpē Heights on Kauaʻi and has been battling rose beetles for the last five years, made a couple of observations: Infestations seem to be greatest after a heavy rain—in the few weeks following, all his trees, even a tall tangerine, are hit relentlessly. Since the last summer was very dry, beetles have not been a major problem. He figures that the beetles are coming out of his own lawn or the cane field. If he needs to get his plants in prime condition, he moves them from the nursery into the backyard, where floodlights are installed. He turns on the lights at sunset and leaves them on for about two hours. Under these conditions, he has zero beetle damage to even the most susceptible plants.

De Motta has susceptible plants at the front of his house, where there is a streetlight. During major infestations, they do get hit but not that severely. He has treated many of my plants with Merit, and although it doesn't stop the beetles outright, I find they don't feed so vigorously as to cause major damage.

Again, this is all based on the fact that major infestations occur for him after major rains. So they are cyclical. If his planted material is healthy, the beetle damage usually doesn't affect the vigor of the plant. And that is the main thing. We can consider some beetle damage acceptable even though it doesn't look nice. Once the cycle is over, the plants grow out of it. If you can avoid spraying insecticides and using nitrogen fertilizers, the plants will be tough and look natural.

Growing Native Hawaiian Plants

We are striving for a balance in the garden. Do not use too much commercial fertilizer; some of the best gardeners use NO fertilizer, just 'ōpala recycled from the garden. Nitrogen, especially, can produce overlush and succulent growth that just provides a lū'au for pests.

Dr. Adrian Brash had an epic garden up Tantalus. We got to visit him with Susan and Ashby Fritso. I asked Dr. Brash (who was about eighty at the time and had just finished mowing his one-acre lot), what kind of fertilizer he used. Everything was so lush and healthy.

"'Ōpala," he answered. "'Ōpala?" "Yes, I use leaves, banana trunks, mixed grass clippings, and other 'ōpala from the yard to nourish and sustain the garden." Seeing is believing and I have used more 'ōpala and less chemical fertilizer ever since.

Another great gardener with a garden in balance is Leland Miyano of Kahalu'u. He never uses fertilizer and, more important, he has never used heavy equipment on his land. The soil has not been scraped and compacted and hauled away, as a result of house construction and building techniques, the way most home garden soil has been. Miyano loves using rocks and giant boulders to enhance garden design, and he moves them in ingenious ways, without a crane and bulldozer, which would ruin his perfectly built up organic soil structure.

JoAnne Pinney gardens professionally on Kaua'i, and as a surfer she is very conscious of what goes into her gardens. She knows that any overspray will end up in Hanalei Bay. She uses bone meal, blood meal, green sand, and other natural, soil-building, environmentally friendly products.

Alfalfa pellets are another excellent plant builder. You can add alfalfa pellets to plants in the ground or in pots. Pinney puts a couple in the crown of hāpu'u tree fern and waters them in well. Tree fern trunks are basically all roots, so feeding them with alfalfa works well. (It can attract flies, so be prepared for that.) Fish emulsion also smells and can attract insects, but only temporarily.

Small amounts of fertilizers are necessary, but as experienced gardeners will note, using too much nitrogen for native Hawaiian plants produces lush growth and makes them attractive to chewing insects. Natural fertilizers such as fish emulsion and kelp at half the recommended strength, applied during active growing periods, and slow-release fertilizers (e.g., Osmocote) can work well.

Trees such as koa, koai'a, 'ohai, māmane, and wiliwili capture nitrogen from the air. Plant other plants near or under them. The nitrogen-fixing plants are designed to gather, or "fix," nitrogen from the air and supply it to the soil, and surrounding plants thrive from the free nitrogen.

Leaves (phyllodes) from trees in the bean family, like monkeypod, showers, and poinciana, and natives like koa and koai'a make great mulch. Let the leaves fall or place them around other plants in the garden. As the leaves break down they do all the good things for the soil and water and plants that any mulch does and they slowly release nitrogen into the ground. It's free, clean, and natural.

Tree chips produced when tree trimmers cut and grind trees and

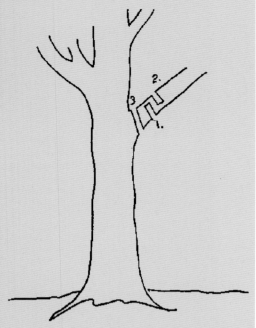

**LIMB REMOVAL USING THE
1-2-3-CUT METHOD**
*Make cuts in this order to avoid bark
rips and splits when pruning large,
heavy branches.*

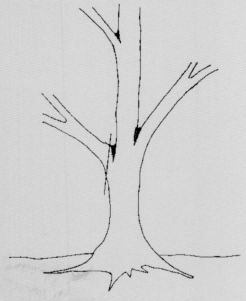

BRANCH COLLAR
*The branch collar is a zone of corky-
looking, rapidly growing "healing cells"
found around the crotch of branches.
Make your pruning cut at least an inch
out from and parallel to this zone so the
tree can use its natural defenses to close
off the pruning wound.*

logs can be great for the garden. Different kinds of wood can be used for different purposes. Coconut, *hau*, monkeypod, or shower trimmings are great for general garden use. Hardwoods like iron-wood and eucalyptus can be used at garden bed edges to prevent weeds. These slowly decompose and last longer than the softer *hau*, *niu*, etc. After they break down you can mix them into the general compost on garden beds.

Stone mulch is a great tool. We have all kinds of rock depending on the look you want. Blue rock makes a lovely, long-lasting top dressing. I prefer black or red cinders depending on the colors in the plant pallet. Coral chips are great for beach gardens and very nurturing for coastal native plants.

My old roommate Erin Lee and I were first taught stone mulching by Ruth Hanner up in her Kōke‘e garden on Kaua‘i. She had been taught this technique as a young farmer's wife in Peru. She had us dress up her *poha* patch with stones after we had it all weeded.

PRUNING

Pruning is an important horticultural technique. You can shape and size your plants and direct their growth, and by pruning in a careful and studied way, you can get cuttings to grow new plants for yourself or for your family and friends.

To prune ground covers, shrubs, and vines, use a sharp pair of clean clippers (sterilize them with a flame or rubbing alcohol before cutting a new plant so you won't spread plant diseases).

The basic rule of pruning is to study the plant before you do any cutting. Cutting is easy, but its effect on the plant may be radical, so take your time and step back and look every so often. Above where each leaf attaches to the stem (the internode), there is a bud. This bud has the potential to grow into a new stem or branch. To control direction, pick a bud facing the way you want the plant to grow and cut off the stem above it. The new bud will grow in that direction.

Pruning of trees and woody shrubs requires a sharp hand saw, loppers, or even a chain saw. All these should be used with caution, for your own safety and that of the plant.

The rules of pruning that many of us grew up learning have changed. From doing "autopsies" on failed trees, we have discovered that some of the old methods are harmful. No longer do we make flush cuts, use pruning paint, or top trees if they get too big.

If a tree is too big, we cut it back to the next branch, never just whack it off in the middle of the branch. We look at the natural growth and form of the tree and prune it accordingly.

Every tree has a branch collar. We find this and use it to decide where to make the cut. The branch collar is where healing, partitioning cells are formed. We make the cut out from and parallel to the collar so the tree can close off the wound from the cut.

After cutting we use no pruning paint or other wound dressing. Leaving the cut open to oxygen lets the cells close off the wound.

PLANTING OUT

Put most native Hawaiian plants in a sunny location, in soil that is well drained. Make the planting hole twice as wide as the root ball or present pot, and as deep. If the soil is claylike and drains slowly, mix in some coarse red or black cinder, perlite, or coarse compost. Place some slow-release fertilizer in the bottom of the hole. Carefully remove the plant from the container and put it in the hole. The top of the medium should be at the same level as the top of the hole. If it sits too high or too low, make the hole deeper or shallower so the plant is at the right depth. Water thoroughly after you transplant.

Planting with the aid of the moon is not hard. Old farmers watch the moon and so did the ancient Hawaiians. The late May Moir taught me some simple horticulture guidelines:

- For cuttings, plant on the waning moon.
- For seeds, pollination, etc., plant on the waxing moon.

Some people laugh at this method, but we have found that with difficult, rare, and precious native Hawaiian plants, being aware of and following the moon phases does help the plants to grow.

WATER GARDENING WITH NATIVES

Dear Heidi,

Are there some natives that can be used in the new and old craze of water gardening?

Chip Hartman, Pūpūkea

YES! Many native grasses and sedges can be used. Some native ferns, like *ʻihi ʻihi lauakea* (our native four-leaf-clover–looking endangered fern), need water for at least part of their life cycle. *Neke* and *hōʻiʻo* are two Polynesian-introduced water ferns that do well in water gardens. *Neke* is gorgeous where submersed. *Makaloa* (native sedge), from which fine mats are made, does well in brackish water. Another suitable sedge is *puʻukaʻa*.

Make a *hapa-haole* water garden using *kalo*, vibrant water lilies, lotus—whatever you have the imagination and room for. *Bacopa*, or *ʻae ʻae*, is a good wet-loving ground cover or water garden plant. Versatile and tough, it has nice small leaves and bluish flowers. We grew it at Hoʻomaluhia Botanical Garden for native *koloa* (ducks) that were reintroduced there.

NATIVES AS POTTED PLANTS

Many people don't have land to work; fortunately, many natives grow well in pots, especially shrubs and ground covers and plants from coastal or dry regions. Many ferns do well in pots and are suitable for more shady areas.

The larger the better, as far as pots for long-term growing are concerned. Get a big ceramic or clay decorative pot that adds to your décor and fill it with native plants for some unique landscaping.

Remember that you must water plants in pots more often than the same plants in the ground because their roots can't spread out the way field-planted plants can. Even if the plant is drought tolerant or less thirsty and "never" needs water, you need to water it when it's planted in a pot.

If you're growing potted plants on a lanai, take the amount of light into account. Some lanais don't get much sunlight; others have baking, late-afternoon sun. You need to grow the types of plants that will thrive in the light your lanai gets.

You can set up an automatic irrigation system even on a lanai. This might be handy when you go on vacation if you don't have a reliable "plant sitter."

NATIVES AS HOUSEPLANTS

Shade-loving native plants have potential in the home, office, and hotel lobby as well as in other interiorscapes. Some people—notably Senji of Pat's Island Delights and Jeff Preble of Pisces Pacifica, as well as Rick Barboza and Matt Kapaliku Schirman of Hui Kū Maoli Ola Nursery in Waimānalo—have been testing some such as *pāpala*. I tested this in my office as well, and it thrived and was very interesting to visitors to the Honolulu Botanical Garden.

My friend Jackie Ralya has a long-lived *palapalai* fern in her bathroom. It looks and smells great and lends beauty to her interior spaces.

BASIC LANDSCAPE MAINTENANCE

Landscape maintenance of native Hawaiian plants requires something you probably already have lots of: common sense. Observe your plants and try to determine what they need. We have so many different kinds of soil in Hawai'i that a hard-and-fast rule for watering, soil amending, or mulching is not available. Look at your plants and feel the soil to see if you need to water.

Find out where and how native plants grow in the wild. Go hiking and see where plants grow. Consult experts in the field and use Hawaiian reference books. Observe the plants in botanical and private gardens and see how they are grown there. Ask the gardeners how they grow their plants. Try to duplicate the wild or best cultivated conditions for the plants you choose to grow. Although we like to try to grow everything in Hawai'i, it is best to select plants suited to our environment. If you live near the beach and it is hot and dry, coastal and dry forest plants will grow best for you. If you live in a cool, moist shady area, grow plants from moist and rain forest habitats.

We can still "have it all" though, if we insist. Plants from the lowlands can often be grown well in moister, mauka settings. Just be sure to protect the dryland plants from too much rain, select a full-sun site for them, and make sure the soil drains well.

It is not as easy to grow plants from upland or rain forest areas in lowland hot gardens. You can select the most sheltered and shady corner of your garden, add lots of rich organic matter to the soil, and water frequently.

Some commonsense ideas apply to most plants: Don't hit the trunk or base of a plant with a lawnmower or weed trimmer. No plant thrives after getting its bark stripped off.

Make sure the soil drains well. Do the "hose test": apply water with a hose or bucket and see how fast it soaks down into the soil; if it seems to pool there and not drain in a minute or two, you probably need to improve the drainage. Incorporate coarse rock, cinder, or compost; mound the soil up, break it up with tools or with organic fertilizers and compost.

If the soil seems too coarse and sandy, you may have to add organics to improve its fertility and water-holding capacity. Many native Hawaiian plants like a coarse, sandy, well-drained soil, but in these conditions, and also during very dry or windy periods, you will have to water more to get the plants established.

To mulch or not to mulch—that is an important question with native Hawaiian plants. One thing that is apparent to Hawaiian gardeners is that mulch and other organics do not work the same here as in other places. Our hot, humid conditions year round mean that organic mulches break down and decay rapidly. You spend hours gathering and hauling organic mulches up and into your garden, faithfully apply them, and then in a few months there is no visible sign of mulch. Do the menehune come down and steal the mulch at night? No, it just has broken down and become a part of the soil.

Thick organic mulches can also be a hiding place for such pests as slugs and Chinese rose beetles. Never pile up mulch right next to the stem or trunk of a plant; keep it a few inches away.

I prefer stone mulches for their attractiveness, permanence, and soil-improvement qualities. We have many attractive stone types here in Hawai'i. Red or black cinders, blue rock chips, smooth river rocks, and coral chips are some of our choice natural materials.

GROUND COVERS

'Ākia *fruit are an attractive landscape addition, nice in leis. You can easily pop the seed out of the fruit and plant it to grow new* 'ākia.

Growing ground covers rather than turf grass in parts of your landscape is a great way to reduce maintenance (mostly lawn mowing) and water use. Ground covers can also add to the interest and aesthetics of your yard. People who live in high rises can grow ground covers in large pots if they water them regularly.

'ĀKIA

SCIENTIFIC NAME: *Wikstroemia uva–ursi*
FAMILY: Thymelaeaceae ('ākia family)

Endemic

'Ākia is a small, sprawling ground cover. It has oval waxy green leaves arranged in an overlapping pattern. Flowers are small, four-parted and yellowish green, and they usually bloom in clusters. Flowers are followed by orange-red berries. 'Ākia grows to heights of 1 to 3 feet, but it mainly spreads laterally. Some old plants are as wide across as 10 feet.

PROPAGATION AND CARE: 'Ākia can be grown from seeds, cuttings, or air-layers. Seeds are the easiest for the home gardener. Collect ripe red seeds. Squeeze the seed out of the pulp and plant it in a pot of clean potting mix. Cover with about 1/4 inch of medium and water daily. Transplant seedlings at the two-leaf stage.

Cuttings require wounding (making vertical slices with a knife or stripping some bark so the hormones can penetrate better), strong rooting hormones, and a mist system to grow. Air-layers are used by commercial nurseries to produce larger plants fairly quickly. Home gardeners who are skilled in air-layering may also want to use this technique to make big plants.

Handsomely cascading over this hollow-tile wall in Enchanted Lakes, O'ahu, is a groundcover planting of 'ākia.

LANDSCAPE USE: 'Ākia is a good ground cover or low shrub. To grow it as an effective ground cover, plant the young plants 1 foot on center (a foot apart) or closer. It is lovely sprawling over a stone wall, embankment, or rocks. 'Ākia is very drought and wind tolerant, once established. Thus it is a great plant for water-saving gardening, or xeriscaping. Here in Hawai'i we can call it "akamai wai gardening."

PESTS: 'Ākia has very few pests or problems.

OTHER USES: The flowers and the orange-red fruit are prized (along with some of the leafy twigs) for making *lei haku*.

'Ākia is one of the few native Hawaiian plants used as a poison. The early Hawaiians found out that it is a cold-blooded poison, so they were able to catch fish using extracts of 'ākia. They ground up its twigs and cast them into the water of a tidepool or fishpond. Or they sometimes took a basket full of pounded 'ākia, weighted it with stones, and placed the basket in an enclosed body of water. Stunned fish were then easy to catch, but the fishermen or the fish eaters weren't harmed because humans are warm blooded. This use has given it another common name: the "fish poison plant."

'ILIMA PAPA
SCIENTIFIC NAME: *Sida fallax*
FAMILY: Malvaceae (hibiscus family)

Indigenous to Hawai'i and all Pacific islands to China

'Ilima papa is a low ground cover (6 to 12 inches tall). Its bright yellow flowers look like miniature hibiscus (to which it is related).

PROPAGATION AND CARE: *'Ilima papa* is easily grown from seeds or cuttings. It responds well to fertilizer, especially foliar types, while it is being grown in the nursery or landscape.

LANDSCAPE USE: *'Ilima papa* makes a good ground cover in a hot, sunny location.

PESTS: Sucking and chewing insects can sometimes be a problem if the plants are stressed, but this can be handled with standard insecticides.

OTHER USES: The flowers are made into leis and represent the island of O'ahu. It takes about a thousand of the delicate, ephemeral blossoms to make one strand of a lei. Lei makers have a saying that you should "pick the fragile blossoms before the sun shines on their golden faces."
    The buds are used to quench thirst on hot, dusty hikes through areas where *'ilima* grows. They are also used as a mild, good-tasting (and fun to take) laxative, especially for keiki. *'Ilima papa* is a fibrous plant and has been used to weave quick baskets.

KOLOKOLO KAHAKAI, *PŌHINAHINA,* BEACH *VITEX*
SCIENTIFIC NAME: *Vitex rotundifolia*
FAMILY: Verbenaceae (verbena family)

Indigenous to Hawai'i, other Pacific islands, China, Taiwan, Japan, Southeast Asian islands, India, Sri Lanka, Mauritius, Australia
Kolokolo kahakai is a ground cover, or sprawling shrub, 6 inches to 2 feet tall. It spreads laterally and grows rapidly once established. It

As you can see from this close-up, 'ilima flowers look like miniature hibiscus. 'Ilima is the lei flower of O'ahu.

Kolokolo kahakai *has lovely lavender flowers.*

Kolokolo kahakai *grows on the beach at Waialua, on the north shore of O'ahu. Neighbors must sandbag against high surf and storm waves. These protective natives allow adjacent homeowners to relax and go surfing; their beach won't wash away.*

Pā'ū-o-Hi'iaka's *flowers are either blue or white.*

has silvery oval leaves, sometimes with a tinge of lavender near the margins. The foliage has a spicy fragrance. Flowers are about 1 inch long, lavender, and clustered near the tips of the stems. Fruits are round, about 1/4 inch across, and green tinged with brown and lavender.

PROPAGATION AND CARE: *Kolokolo kahakai* can be propagated from seeds or cuttings, but cuttings are faster. Cuttings stuck directly in the ground and watered daily with a soaker hose for about three weeks have been reported to grow. This was in old, red sugarcane soil.

LANDSCAPE USE: *Kolokolo kahakai* makes a good ground cover or potted specimen. It is salt and wind tolerant, tough and persistent in most landscapes. It grows well in sandy soils and, surprisingly for a beach plant, it does well in red clay soils as well. It thrives over a broad range of elevations. It makes a good plant for the inland/upland xeriscape. Because it tends to sprawl, it is attractive cascading over rock walls or scrambling over boulders and rocks in the landscape. It is a good cover for fairly steep banks. It has been reported to do well in large clay or cement pots on a sunny lanai. It needs full sun. As long as the soil is fairly well drained, it will thrive. Water well for the first few weeks and then taper off as the plant gets established.

PESTS: *Kolokolo kahakai* has few pests or problems.

OTHER USES: *Kolokolo kahakai* is attractive when used in leis. The colors of silvery green highlighted with lavender are striking, and the spicy fragrance of the foliage adds another dimension to your lei.

PĀ'Ū-O-HI'IAKA

SCIENTIFIC NAME: *Jacquemontia ovalifolia* subsp. *sandwicensis*
FAMILY: Convolvulaceae (morning glory family)

Endemic

Pā'ū-o-Hi'iaka is a sprawling ground cover, 3 to 8 inches tall, with pale blue or white blossoms. It usually stays low to the ground. Leaves are small to medium in size (about 3 inches long and 1 inch wide), and the flowers are about 1 inch wide. Seed capsules follow the flowers. The capsules are tan and papery and contain several small, brown-black seeds.

PROPAGATION AND CARE: *Pā'ū-o-Hi'iaka* is easy to propagate from cuttings or seeds. To grow it from cuttings, take a two- or three-node cutting (about 3 or 4 inches long). Stick about one-third of the cutting in a pot of potting medium and water it daily. Most well-drained media will work for propagation, and rooting hormone is not needed for cuttings.

To grow *pā'ū-o-Hi'iaka* from seeds, plant the seeds (there are several tiny seeds to each brown papery seed capsule) on firm premoistened potting medium. Barely cover the seeds with medium and firm this covering down with another clean pot. Water daily. Suggested potting medium is one part perlite, one part peat moss, and one part black or red cinder.

LANDSCAPE USE: *Pā'ū-o-Hi'iaka* makes an effective and interesting ground cover, especially if interplanted with other native ground covers like *'ilima*, *'ohai*, *'ākia*, and *kolokolo kahakai*. We call this type of interplanting a "Hawaiian tapestry" groundcover planting. *Pā'ū-o-Hi'iaka* will also do well in a large pot or a hanging basket.

PESTS: Few pests and diseases have been reported on *pā'ū-o-Hi'iaka*.

HOW *PĀ'Ū-O-HI'IAKA* GOT ITS NAME: Pele, the volcano goddess, loved her baby sister Hi'iaka very much and took her everywhere. In hula chants you will hear, "*Hi'iaka i ka poli o Pele*" (Hi'iaka in the bosom of Pele)—Hi'iaka was so small when she came from Kahiki that she was only an egg, and Pele kept her warm in her bosom or armpit. One day, a very long time ago, Pele took Hi'iaka with her to the beach. The waves were up, the fishing was good, and Pele went out into the water, leaving baby Hi'iaka on the beach. The waves got bigger and better, the fish were biting like crazy, and Pele kept staying out in the water. The sun was getting hotter and hotter, too. On the beach, baby Hi'iaka was uncomfortable and getting all *papa'a* (burned). The gods and a little viny beach plant with blue flowers felt sorry for Hi'iaka, so the vine quickly grew over Hi'iaka and protected her from the harsh Hawaiian sun. That is how it got the name *pā'ū* (a skirt, or woman's garment) of Hi'iaka.

NEHE

SCIENTIFIC NAME: *Lipochaeta integrifolia*
FAMILY: Asteraceae (sunflower family)

Endemic

Nehe is a small, sprawling plant, 6 to 8 inches tall, with small, succulent leaves and yellow daisylike flowers. The leaves have a silvery-gray appearance, or they can be quite green in a moist setting.

PROPAGATION AND CARE: *Nehe* is easy to grow from cuttings, with or without mist, in just about any well-drained medium. Rooting hormone is not essential to successful propagation.

LANDSCAPE USE: *Nehe* makes an excellent ground cover. It has been suggested as a replacement for the overused *Wedelia*, but it is not quite as easy to grow.

PESTS: Some of the sucking insects, such as mealy bugs, sometimes attack *nehe*. Standard insecticides may be used (wettable powder formulation is best). Newly introduced slime bugs sometimes attack the

A blooming "Hawaiian tapestry planting" of blue-flowered pā'ū-o-Hi'iaka *and golden-flowered* 'ilima

Nehe, *a native yellow-flowered daisy, happily cascades over rocks or makes a nice ground cover.*

new growth of *nehe*. Smash these by hand (the slime makes it hard for chemicals to penetrate down to the bug itself) and then spray the plant with insecticidal soap or insecticide.

OTHER USES: There are many species of *nehe* in Hawai'i. *Lipochaeta integrifolia* is the most like a ground cover, but many other attractive bush or shrublike members of this genus can be grown in Hawai'i gardens.

HINAHINA

SCIENTIFIC NAME: *Heliotropium anomalum*
FAMILY: Boraginaceae (*kou* family)

Indigenous to Hawai'i and most of Polynesia

Hinahina is a small coastal Hawaiian plant. In the wild it grows from 1 to 8 inches tall. In cultivation it usually grows from 6 to 8 inches tall. The foliage is very silvery (*hinahina*, in the Hawaiian language), somewhat succulent, with leaves clustered in tight rosettes. It has tiny white fragrant flowers.

PROPAGATION AND CARE: *Hinahina* can be grown from cuttings, with or without mist. A good potting mix is one part black or red cinder, one part peat moss, and two parts perlite.

LANDSCAPE USE: *Hinahina* makes a beautiful silvery ground cover that is tolerant of drought, salt, and wind once established in the landscape. It grows to 3 to 12 inches tall in cultivation. It seems to hold up well in the landscape. It requires full sun. Although *hinahina* grows naturally in very dry areas, it needs regular watering in cultivation, especially if grown in a pot. Although it will get more succulent and silvery with less water, do not let it get so dry that it wilts. Experiment with water in your own landscape. The less water you give it, the more silvery and succulent it will be.

PESTS: Mealy bugs sometimes attack *hinahina*. Do not overfertilize, because the succulent growth produced is attractive to insects. Insecticidal soap or standard insecticide (wettable powder formulation is best, e.g., Sevin, Malathion) can be used. *Hinahina* sometimes dies back. This might be from inconsistent watering, or perhaps from a fungal or root disease. We need to grow this plant more to find out what it really needs to thrive in the landscape.

OTHER USES: *Hinahina* is the flower and lei of the island of Kaho'olawe. The flowers and leafy rosettes are prized for *lei haku*. The whole leafy tip of the plant, with or without the flowers, is plucked from the plant. The growing number of people who like to make *hinahina* leis are threatening the plant they admire. *Hinahina* is becoming more and more rare at the coastal sites where it is native. Happily, though, *hinahina* has proved fairly easy to grow. Cuttings are a good method of propagation.

Hinahina *leaves grow in a dense silvery rosette pattern that is gorgeous and striking, even with no flowers present.*

The fragrant flowers of hinahina, *along with the silvery twigs, are fashioned into the lei of Kaho'olawe.*

'IHI

SCIENTIFIC NAME: *Portulaca* spp.
FAMILY: Portulacaceae (purslane family)

Endemic (*Portulaca molokiniensis, Portulaca sclerocarpa, Portulaca villosa*)
Indigenous to Hawai'i and the Pacific from New Caledonia to Pitcairn Island , Polynesia and Micronesia (*Portulaca lutea*)
Naturalized (*Portulaca oleracea, Portulaca pilosa, Portulaca*)

The clustered blossoms of Portulacca molokiniensis

Portulacas are small, usually succulent herbs. There are seven native Hawaiian species. There is also a weedy, natural red portulaca found in Hawai'i, the purslane, *P. oleracea* (pigweed), and a cultivated introduction, the moss rose, *P. grandiflora. Portulaca lutea* has yellow, single-petaled flowers with one to three flowers blooming at the tips of the stems. The anthers of the flowers range in color from yellow to red. This species is indigenous; it is found on other Pacific islands in Polynesia and Micronesia, as well as on shores and coastlines of the Northwestern Hawaiian Islands and on O'ahu, Moloka'i, Lāna'i, Maui, and Hawai'i. *Portulaca molokiniensis* is a recently discovered endemic species that grows on the offshore islets of Molokini and Pu'ukoa'e, and at Kamōhio Bay, Kaho'olawe. It was described by State of Hawai'i forester Bob Hobdy, who did a survey of the flora of the offshore islands of Maui County. It has very succulent, overlapping leaves that give the plant an attractive and interesting appearance. The round, corky stems with their succulent leaves stand more upright than in most other portulacas. The plants can reach a height of about 12 inches. The flowers are lemon yellow and are found in clusters at the tips of the leaves. When the plant is going to flower, it sends a leafless, flower-bearing stem above the succulent leaves. *Portulaca villosa* has pale grayish-green, narrow leaves. Three to six flowers are found at the tips of the stems. They are white, pink, or pink with white centers. They grow naturally on dry, rocky, clay or coral sites on Nihoa, Ka'ula, and all the main islands except Kaua'i and Ni'ihau. *Portulaca* sp. nova is an undescribed species that is very rare. It has been found only in Olowalu Valley on the west side of Maui. This is a dry valley that is threatened by the rampant development in the area. This species has pale pink flowers with a white center, and yellow anthers.

Portulaca *sp.* nova, *from Olowalu, Maui, is very rare, but easy to grow.*

PROPAGATION AND CARE: The Hawaiian portulacas are easy to grow. The succulent cuttings root easily, and rooting hormones and mist systems are not necessary. Cuttings 2 to 5 inches long, with the lower leaves removed, are stuck in a pot of potting mix. With daily watering they root easily in a couple of weeks. Portulacas can also be grown from seed. The seeds are very tiny, round and brown or black. The hardest trick can be finding the seeds before they are lost in the dirt. Sow them on firm, premoistened medium in a clean pot. Barely cover the tiny seeds, and firm the medium again. Water

Portulacca molokininensis *at Wailea, Maui. Note the succulent leaves, growing in an attractive imbricate pattern. This is a striking plant for xeric gardens or xeriscapes.*

carefully, for the tiny seeds are easily washed to one side or out of the pot.

LANDSCAPE USE: Portulacas make a good ground cover, either alone or mixed with other coastal groundcover plants to create a "Hawaiian tapestry" in your landscape. They grow well in pots of well-drained medium set in a sunny location. They also make interesting specimens for the rock garden. They are good candidates for the xeriphytic, water-saving garden by virtue of their succulent nature. *Portulaca molokiniensis* is a striking specimen plant, with its unusual growth habit and spikes of bright gold flowers. The ornamental portulacas are heavy feeders. They require regular fertilization to maintain a thick mat as a ground cover and to bloom consistently. The Hawaiian species are generally similar in this requirement. Fertilize regularly with slow-release organic fertilizer (e.g., Complehumus 8–8–8 or fish emulsion) or with liquid foliar fertilizer (e.g., Miracle-Gro). Follow the directions on the fertilizer label.

PESTS: Few pests are known for portulacas. Overwatering should be avoided (as with all succulent plants) to avoid rot.

ʻŪLEI

SCIENTIFIC NAME: *Osteomeles anthyllidifolia*
FAMILY: Rosaceae (rose family)

Indigenous to Hawaiʻi, the Cook Islands, and Tonga

This ʻūlei thrives clambering over the boulders along the Kuliʻouʻou Trail, Oʻahu, in a very dry area.

ʻŪlei has glossy green leaves, flexible stems, and clusters of white, gently fragrant blossoms, followed by white round fruit with a bluish tint. It is one of the toughest and most versatile of our native plants. You find it in places that have been almost totally taken over by aggressive alien weeds. Roadsides where nothing native is left will sometimes sport some ʻūlei twining around the other plants quite happily. In the wild you find it in open, sunny places where the wind whips by, along slopes and roadsides, and clambering up the other plants in dry to moist forested lands. You can see ʻūlei along many of our popular hiking trails.

ʻŪlei is an indigenous native Hawaiian plant: it got here on its own without help from people, but other plants of the same species grow naturally in other places. ʻŪlei also grows in other parts of Polynesia and in the Bonin and Ryukyu Islands, near Japan.

PROPAGATION AND CARE: ʻŪlei can be grown from seeds or cuttings. Because it is a dry forest plant where rainfall is unpredictable, its seeds will germinate sporadically over a long period of time; this is a good tactic for a plant to survive in a dry place, where consistent rain may or may not come and the offspring have to be prepared for whatever falls from the sky. So be patient if you try to grow it from seeds. The one time I got really good germination from seeds was right after Hurricane 'Iniki. One month after the hurricane I collected some seeds at the urging of my lei-making friend Brian Choy. I told him at the time, "You watch, they'll be sprouting over the next two years." But all the seeds germinated in a month. We think the hurricane shocked them all into being ready to grow right then.

Separate the pulp from the seeds in water. You can soak the seeds in water for a day or two to enhance germination. The seeds are small, so sow them carefully on moist, prefirmed potting medium.

Cuttings should be 2 to 4 inches long. Use rooting hormones and keep them as moist as possible in the first few weeks of rooting.

Fragrant clusters of white blossoms adorn 'ūlei, a native in the rose family. It is a very tough and useful plant.

LANDSCAPE USE: *'Ūlei* is attractive for different uses in many landscapes. It is a nice ground cover, alone or mixed with other low-growing native plants like *'ilima, pā'ū-o-Hi'iaka, hinahina, 'ena'ena,* or flowering exotic annuals. It looks great sprawling over lava or coral boulders or clambering over a low wall. It can be trimmed as a specimen shrub, or plant a few together and make a hedge. The flexible stems can be trained to go where you direct. They can be looped upward for a trellis decoration, or you can grow them up into a tree. With time, *'ūlei* can be trained into a small tree itself. It likes a wide range of growing conditions. It will grow down at the coast or up mauka. It is found naturally from sea level to 4000 feet in elevation. As long as it gets plenty of sun, adequate watering, and well-drained soil, it should thrive.

PESTS: *'Ūlei* has few pests.

OTHER USES: Early Hawaiians used this plant for spears, *'ūkēkē* (a musical instrument), and the hoops of fishnets. The twining woody stems are supple and flexible when young, tough and strong when mature.

'ALA'ALA WAI NUI

SCIENTIFIC NAME: *Peperomia* spp.
FAMILY: Piperaceae (pepper family)

Endemic (23 species)
Indigenous to Hawai'i, Micronesia, Melanesia, Polynesia, and Queensland, Australia (*Peperomia leptostachya*)
Naturalized (*Peperomia pellucida*)

Many species of *Peperomia* grow in Hawai'i. They are usually small herbs with small leaves. The leaves may be green, or green with red markings. The flowers are tiny and come on thin spikes found at the leaf tips. *Peperomia* is related to *'awa,* or *kawa,* and to black pepper. In Hawaiian forests, *Peperomia* can be found perched on the moist trunks of trees, sprawling over rocks and boulders, and sometimes in soil if it is rich and full of organic material. In the garden, it likes a rich but well-drained medium.

'Ala 'ala wai nui from North Hālawa Valley, O'ahu. The shade for this plant was destroyed during freeway construction. We collected and grew it with the help of Jimmy Pang. It is a very attractive shade garden addition.

'Ala'ala wai nui nestles among the moss-covered rocks along this ancient Hawaiian trail at Kalaupapa, Moloka'i.

'Uki'uki growing as specimen shrubs at the Queen Kapi'olani flower garden. The city has planted many natives in this garden, near the zoo and Kapi'olani Park. Note Diamond Head, or Lē'ahi, in the background.

Peat moss, perlite, and black cinder in equal proportions make a good planting medium. Leafy compost also works well.

PROPAGATION AND CARE: *Peperomia* species grow well and easily from cuttings. Either stem or tip cuttings work fine. Make cuttings 3 to 4 inches long, remove the lower leaves, and cut the upper leaves in half. Cut off any flower spikes, since flower growth and seed development take energy away from the plant. You want to channel this energy into root production. You can plant the seed spikes separately and grow the seedlings too. The cuttings do not seem to need rooting hormones. Plant the cuttings about 1/2 inch deep in a half-and-half mixture of peat moss and perlite. Place them in a cool, shady place and water daily or twice daily if you can.

LANDSCAPE USE: *Peperomia* plants are gorgeous on boulders, at the top of stone retaining walls, and as a ground cover for shady or semi-shady areas. They are also attractive potted plants, preferring shade.

PESTS: *Peperomia* is sometimes attacked by fungi that make it rot at the base. Careful attention to watering and drainage can help prevent this. You can also spray with a standard fungicide if you notice the problem. If the plants start to rot, they can sometimes be saved by rooting tip cuttings as outlined above.

OTHER USES: The early Hawaiians made a gray *kapa* dye from *Peperomia*.

'UKI'UKI

SCIENTIFIC NAME: *Dianella sandwicensis*
FAMILY: Liliaceae (lily family)

Indigenous

'Uki'uki is a native Hawaiian clump-forming lily. It is found in dry and mesic forests, in open sunny places at the edge of the deep forest. It has handsome strap-shaped leaves, growing in a cluster. The flowers are a bright blue, with contrasting yellow stamens. When pollinated, the flowers form blue berries with seeds inside.

PROPAGATION AND CARE: *'Uki'uki* is easy to grow from seeds, or you can divide a large clump into smaller chunks and replant those in a pot or directly into the ground.

LANDSCAPE USE: *'Uki'uki* is attractive in the landscape as an accent plant (the blue flowers and fruit provide unusual interest and contrast). The clumps make a nice grouped planting or understory for trees and shrubs, and do well on banks and slopes. The plants grow to about 3 feet tall and as wide or wider in the garden. They can also be grown in large decorative pots.

Growing Native Hawaiian Plants

PESTS: This is a fairly pest-resistant plant. Scale and aphid insects sometimes attack the leaves. These can be controlled with insecticidal soap and removal by hand.

OTHER USES: A blue dye for *kapa* was made from the berries. The long, strong leaves were sometimes used for the inside thatch of *hale*.

'AKOKO

SCIENTIFIC NAMES: *Chamaesyce celastroides, C. skottsbergii, C. degeneri*
FAMILY: Euphorbiaceae

Endemic

'*Akoko* is found on sandy shorelines, in dryland forests, and in mesic (intermediately wet) forests. There are several species of Hawaiian '*akoko*. It is a pretty plant with an interesting leaf arrangement. Often the leaves have a blush or touch of red. '*Akoko* has a milky sap, like other members of this plant family. The flowers are small and develop into fruit capsules with 2 to 3 seeds inside. The fruit capsules are another attractive feature.

'*Akoko* is a tough, drought- and wind-tolerant plant. The coastal species like '*ehukai* (salty) air. '*Akoko* grows in some rugged, harsh coastal environments with battering salt-filled winds and salty, sandy soil, and in dry forests on wind-whipped ridges, in poor soil.

'Akoko *and* 'ae'ae *growing in a striking natural display, against a lava boulder.* 'Akoko *is a great xeriscape plant. Photo by Liz Huppman.*

PROPAGATION AND CARE: Grow '*akoko* from fresh seeds. Try to collect them just as the capsules split open. You can also grow them from small tip cuttings. Seeds are more environmentally friendly and produce plants with stronger root systems.

Establish a "mother plant" in your garden or nursery, and when it is thriving, take cuttings. Not only does this protect plants in the wild, but cuttings from cultivated plants also often root far faster and more easily than cuttings taken from wild plants.

LANDSCAPE USE: This is an excellent plant for sandy beachside gardens. It also thrives in black sand or cinders. It is attractive as a ground cover, as a feature in a rock garden, or as a potted specimen. Like '*ākia* it looks good draped over walls, tumbling over boulders, or anywhere in the garden.

'Akoko *and* 'aki'aki *grass growing in clean beach sand. Note the striking leaf arrangement and red seeds, just beckoning to be eaten and spread by Hawaiian birds.*

PESTS: Sucking insects like scales, mealybugs, and whiteflies sometimes infest '*akoko*. Ants often "farm" the scale and mealies. Control all these pests with insecticidal soap, hand removal, or standard insecticides.

NANEA, BEACH PEA

SCIENTIFIC NAME: *Vigna marina*
FAMILY: Fabaceae (bean family)

Indigenous

Nanea is a yellow-flowered beach pea, which also does well in more upland gardens. It has 3-winged leaves and clusters of yellow flowers borne on separate flower spikes. The flowers form into bean pod–like seed pods, about 2 inches long, with many small, brown round seeds inside.

PROPAGATION AND CARE: Grow *nanea* from seeds. They are very easy to grow and don't require scarification or growing in a pot first. You can sow the seeds directly in the ground where you want a ground cover. Once you have plants growing, flowering, and seeding, *nanea* will self-sow and grow new plants for you naturally, as it would in a large restoration planting like that of the Waimānalo Stream restoration project.

LANDSCAPE USE: In your garden, *nanea* makes a handsome, if short-lived ground cover (keep resowing the seeds where you want them to grow, as you would with a flowering annual plant), with its glossy green leaves and bright blossoms. You can grow it in a pot or hanging basket. It is good on steep slopes and will thrive in many soil types, from sand to compacted clay. *Nanea* will also happily grow as a vine on a support, trellis, or chain link fence.

PESTS: If *nanea* is grown with too much chemical fertilizer, especially nitrogen, it becomes overly lush, and sucking insects and slugs will attack it. *Nanea* is sometimes attacked by mites; spray the underside with soap and water to discourage them.

OTHER USES: *Nanea* is a nitrogen-fixing plant that extracts this essential nutrient from the air with the *kōkua* of symbiotic bacteria. Thus it is a good soil-enriching green manure crop that can be used in organic farming or to naturally enrich the soil for other native or garden plants. You can make a lei from the small yellow flowers or from the seeds.

PAʻINIU

SCIENTIFIC NAME: *Astelia* spp.
FAMILY: Liliaceae (lily family)

This rain forest lily has gorgeous silver leaves, growing in a rosette shape, that are prized by lei makers. Feral pigs love to eat *paʻiniu*. The presence of *paʻiniu* in the forest, especially large clumps on the ground, indicates a healthy forest with few pigs. If you see *paʻiniu* growing only up in the trees, there are lots of pigs feeding in the area. The plant forms silvery flower spikes, and the flowers develop into small, light orange fruits after pollination.

Nanea in golden bloom on a Hawaiʻi beach. This plant will grow from seeds or cuttings in sandy or clay soil. It is a nitrogen-fixing plant with enthusiastic roots that help aerate and enrich the soil. You can plant the seeds where you want them to grow or you can let the plant reseed itself naturally. Photo by Kim and Forrest Starr.

Paʻiniu is a silvery-leafed rain forest lily. Growing this prized lei plant in our gardens is a wise way to perpetuate this precious plant.

LANDSCAPE USE: *Pa'iniu* is not yet widely grown in the landscape, but it has great potential as an accent plant, in a lei garden, or growing up in a tree the way we grow orchids, bromeliads, and epiphytic cacti. The silvery leaves would be a great feature in your moonlit garden.

PROPAGATION AND CARE: *Pa'iniu* is easy to grow from fresh, ripe seeds. It does better at higher elevations, in shady, moist conditions.

PESTS: The biggest pests of this lush lily are feral pigs, goats, and rats. All of these can wipe out *pa'iniu* in an area. Controlling these pests in the forests and cultivating the plants in protected garden sites will help perpetuate this choice plant.

OTHER USES: Lei makers use the leaves as a silvery accent in lei making. They generally fold the leaf over to prominently display the silvery side. In the "old days," having a lei of *Astelia menziesii* from the Volcano area was decorative proof that you had visited the area.

Kahealani Bertelmann wears a lei of pa'iniu *with* liko lehua, *and Pa'ula'ula Hauanio wears a* lei of plain and gorgeous pa'iniu. *Photo by Jean Cote.*

Pa'iniu *perch amidst the mosses and ferns in the* 'ōhi'a lehua *trees of the Kamakou rain and cloud forest on Moloka'i. If there were no feral pigs, they would grow lushly on the ground too.* Pa'iniu, *or* Astelia, *is a lei maker's favorite and a gorgeous plant to nurture and grow in cool upland gardens. Grow it "up a tree" or perched on a garden boulder; with your other epiphytic plants; in rich organic soil in the ground; and in pots in light shade.*

$\mathcal{G}$RASSES AND $\mathcal{S}$EDGES

Q: What do YOU think is the best lawn grass for us hard-working home gardeners? Also, are there any native Hawaiian grasses I can use?

A: Soft-looking, very tough *mānienie*, or good old-fashioned Bermuda grass, is my pick for best looks and ease of maintenance. Just water, fertilize a bit, and mow it and you have a good-looking turf. In wet winters *mānienie* really looks lush and full. In the summer it can look totally dead if you don't water it, but apply water and the deep underground rhizomes send up new fresh grass shoots and it comes right back to lush life.

Native grasses generally aren't the types that make good turf grass; they are more like ornamental bunch grasses. This is a type of gardening that we don't see much in Hawai'i. Thanks to the sugarcane and cattle industries, and good ol' common sense, it's illegal to import grasses without a rigorous quarantine and entry process. Thus we don't have the typical ornamental (i.e., possibly weedy) grasses that mainland landscape designers have for their potential plant palette.

Cultivating a "perfect golf course"–style lawn uses precious resources: water, fresh air, and human labor. Lots of pollutants accompany the pursuit of the perfect lawn: from the fossil fuels for mowers and whackers and for fertilizer manufacture to the runoff of fertilizer, herbicides, and toxic pesticides. I'm an advocate for that lawn style known as mixed Hawaiian green: water, mow, and maybe fertilize, and as long as it's green and fairly thick, it's fine.

Happily we have many native Hawaiian grasses and sedges. Here are some that are showing good potential for landscaping and land restoration:

PILI GRASS

SCIENTIFIC NAME: *Heteropogon contortus*
FAMILY: Poaceae

Indigenous

Pili grass is the proverbial grass of grass shacks. It was used for, among other things, thatching the roofs of Hawaiian *hale*. In the garden it is a tall, 2- to 3-foot bunch grass. It can be very handsome if properly maintained.

A drought- and wind-tolerant plant that can grow in poor and dry soils, *pili* has great potential and should be more widely used in landscape gardens as well as for perpetuating native Hawaiian plants in our forests and shrublands.

Pili is being used to regreen and revegetate the goat-stripped, bombed island of Kahoʻolawe. Fields of *pili* grow on Molokaʻi at the plant materials center (PMC). Robert Joy and his excellent staff are using mechanized harvesting, processing, and growing techniques to restore Hawaiian plants to Kahoʻolawe.

Glenn Sakamoto, PMC manager, is responsible for seed production and has been working closely with Paul Higashino of the Kahoʻolawe Island Reserve Commission (KIRC). Large fields of *pili* are grown in rows like a farmed crop, mechanically harvested, packed into bales of "hay" and then helicoptered to Kahoʻolawe. Joy and Higashino found that leaving the *pili* grass hay in bales provides "nursery" conditions that encourage the *pili* grass to sprout and grow. "Walls" of *pili* bales also serve as a windbreak on the desolate island, capturing moisture and bits of organic matter. The bales can also be set into erosion gullies to slow silt and storm-water runoff. This technique, which has been used on the off-shore islands of Hawaiʻi, provides good nesting habitat for native birds.

Since *pili* grass seeds have a dormancy period, most seeds will not germinate right away. Leaving the grass in bales allows the grass to bide its time, germinate, and then grow in the rich soil formed from the decomposing bale. Restoration specialists working on Kahoʻolawe have seen some *pili* plants growing from the base of the bales.

The Latin species name "*contortus*" refers to the seed heads, which twist and contort. Do not put *pili* grass seeds into your pocket, especially on a damp or rainy day, or you'll be sorry! The seed heads will twist and drill into your moist skin! Ouch!

Pili *grass grows in field rows at the Plant Materials Center at Hoʻolehua, Molokaʻi. Many of the seeds will be baled and sent to Kahoʻolawe for revegetation and land restoration.*

PROPAGATION: Grow *pili* from seeds or divide large clumps and transplant. The seeds have a postharvest dormancy period that's somewhat variable but appears to last 6 to 12 months. Immediately after harvest only 1% to 2% of the seeds will germinate. About 6 months after harvest, germination ranged from 33% to 57% in growing trials at the PMC on Molokaʻi. Germination seems to increase faster if the seeds are not stored under refrigeration.

At the Molokaʻi PMC the seeds are planted in trays under shade cloth and the seedlings are transferred to full sun for a while to "harden up" a bit before they are transplanted in the field. For best results, plant in standard, well-drained potting soil—a commercial potting mix such as Sunshine is fine.

LANDSCAPE USE: *Pili* can be grown in a large pot or in the ground. Plant it amidst landscape boulders or on a dry, windswept slope. Plant it as accent pockets or as a backdrop to more showy or flowering plants. You can use it to revegetate large areas that will be given minimal care once the grass ground cover is established.

Bales of *pili* are excellent for regrowing natives on barren lands.

John Polhemus, wildlife biologist with the Oʻahu District of the Division of Forestry and Wildlife, shared with me how they are using *pili* grass bales to revegetate and reestablish the native seed bank on protected offshore islands like the Mokulua, which are off the coast of Lanikai. They got one shipping pallet of 12 *pili* grass bales and helicoptered them out to the islands. They put a few of them whole into large drainage gullies on the Mokulua Islands. Putting the bales in erosion gullies appeared effective at slowing the rate of downhill storm water flow (and subsequent erosion), and Polhemus and his fellow staffers observed wedge-tailed shearwater chicks nesting underneath the bales. They also broke up several bales and used the "wafers" as mulch for other native plants that they had put out in December 2002. In October 2003, they began to notice scattered *pili* growth across this particular area, with individuals reaching 2 feet tall and loaded with seed. They'd like to continue this treatment, as there are some new (expanding) gullies that need to be plugged, especially after the high and unusual easterly surf and storm waves that hit in November 2003.

OTHER USES/FUN WITH *KEIKI*: A way to "experience" the Latin name of *pili* is to plant some seeds in a pot, apply water, and watch what happens. The seed heads will spiral and twist around as they "drill" the barb-headed seed into the planting media. This is a very "kewl" learning activity for *keiki* of all ages.

KĀWELU, 'EMOLOA, KALAMĀLŌ, LOVE GRASS

SCIENTIFIC NAME: *Eragrostis variabilis*
FAMILY: Graminaceae (also called Poaceae)

Endemic

Kāwelu is an attractive bunch grass that grows well in cultivation. The flower/seed stalks come out green and mature to a golden brown. This is a very drought- and wind-tolerant grass. We saw some the other day on the slopes of *'ihi'ihi lauakea*, above Hanauma Bay. Expert naturalist Jennifer Higashino remarked, "Isn't this gorgeous? It would make a great replacement for weedy [and illegal in Hawai'i] bunch grasses [like the very weedy, fire-loving fountain grass]."

This is one of the grasses that Bob Joy and his staff at the Natural Resources Conservation Service (NRCS) plant material center in Ho'olehua, Moloka'i, are cultivating on a large, mechanized scale for the restoration of Kaho'olawe.

I used to notice it growing gloriously on the steepest *pali* of the Honouliuli Preserve, in the Wai'anae Mountains, far out of reach of the munching goats and pigs. I grew some from seeds, potted them in fairly large pots, and then basically watered and ignored them. Every few months I would stop to admire how tough and handsome the plants were.

Kāwelu grows in rugged, salt-wind conditions on a bluff above Hanauma Bay. This is an attractive grass for gardens and a nice selection for xeriscapes or less thirsty aka-mai-wai *gardening.*

LANDSCAPE USE: This fairly tall and robust grass with the golden seed heads is very attractive in subtle landscapes. Set it amidst boulders, or on a steep slope. Keep it in a large decorative pot, by itself, or in combination with other plants from similar climates.

PROPAGATION AND CARE: Grow *kāwelu* from fresh, ripe seeds. You can also divide large, healthy clumps and repot them in pots on the ground. This makes a long-lived potted plant. It is one of the plants with great utility for land restoration. This hardy grass is being used to regreen Kahoʻolawe and restore the natural Hawaiian ecosystem on the island.

ʻAKIʻAKI

SCIENTIFIC NAME: *Sporobolus virginicus*
FAMILY: Graminaceae (also called Poaeceae)

Indigenous

Akiʻaki, which grows near the coast, is the closest to lawn you will get, but it is a coarse grass that often grows sparsely. It does have good looks though. It grows well in pure sand and makes a nice ground cover (no need to mow!), or you can grow it in a pot. The Pearl City Urban Garden Center has a nice display planting of *akiʻaki*.

It can also grow in well-drained soil in sunny areas. You can let it get as tall as it likes for a rough, grassy ground cover. An example of this is in the plumeria garden at Lāwaʻi Kai, at National Tropical Botanical Garden on Kauaʻi. Hideo Teshima, the late, great gardener, never mowed the grass on a rocky, mildly steep slope under the trees. It looked great and was definitely low-maintenance.

LANDSCAPE USE: Use *akiʻaki* as you would any rambling grass. It works well as erosion control on slopes or on beaches, softening rocks, and as a ground cover with minimal maintenance requirements. Try it in a decorative or terra cotta pot as a wild potted specimen, alone or mixed with other dryland plants.

It looks somewhat like a coarse Bermuda grass, but when you examine it up close (as we must do to identify grasses) you will see that it is quite different. It has golden seed heads, which are very pretty on the coarse grass.

ʻAkiʻaki grass on the beach near shipwrecks on Lānaʻi. It is a very pretty clumping or sparse ground-covering grass. It is good for preventing coastal erosion. Photo by Nathan Yuen.

PROPAGATION AND CARE: *ʻAkiʻaki* is easy to grow from cuttings and divisions. You can also grow it from seeds.

It is very hardy in the landscape, especially if you are in a hot, sandy coastal environment. In more *mauka* areas, provide, as much as possible, well-drained soil and sunlight.

PESTS: *ʻAkiʻaki* has few pests that we know of. Use a light hand with fertilizer and monitor for sucking and chewing insect pests.

Mau'u 'aki'aki, *a petite native sedge, is cute in the garden, attractive among boulders, or suited to pot culture. This is yet another Hawaiian plant with potential in well-designed landscapes and for restoration of native dryland forests and coastal areas. Photo by Liz Huppman.*

Kākonakona *flower head. This grass is velvety and "pettable." Its soft texture and appealing light green color make it suitable for garden installations and sensory gardens. Photo by Liz Huppman.*

Kākonakona *grass with* 'ilima papa *is a simple "garden tapestry" in the wild above* 'Ihi'ihilauākea *or in your own lei garden. Photo by Liz Huppman.*

MAU'U 'AKI'AKI

SCIENTIFIC NAME: *Fimbristylis cymosa*
FAMILY: Cyperaceae

Indigenous

This diminutive sedge is very charming in the garden. It is a low-maintenance plant that is less thirsty and is wind and salt resistant. It is a perfect choice for coastal gardens, poor and sandy soils, and rocky areas.

LANDSCAPE USE: Sand dunes are a natural buffer to high tides and storm waves as well as the rising sea levels from global warming. Most dunes in Hawai'i and other places have been bulldozed or mined. This contributes to the tragic loss of our shorelines.

Sometimes during planning and construction we get a really *akamai* and *'āina*-conscious homeowner as a client. We work for a lovely family like this in Lanikai. They really wanted a pool, for times when there were man-o'-war, or when the ocean was too wild for their *keiki* to comfortably swim in. A huge amount of clean beach sand was excavated for the pool. We convinced the clients to save the sand and make a protective dune/landscape feature on the *makai* side of their property. After some debate with a landscape architect who wanted to do "masses of color," we all agreed to retain the sand and natural coral rubble on the site and do a native coastal dune planting. The plant palette has evolved over time as things flourish and then die back altogether. *Mau'u 'aki'aki* is one of the stalwarts. The original plants are all alive and thriving and expanding in size. Seedlings have sprouted in the coral rubble. It gives a subtle and attractive look to the composition.

PROPAGATION AND CARE: You can grow *mau'u 'aki'aki* from seed or you can divide healthy mature plants. This native sedge is carefree to maintain, once established in the ground.

KĀKONAKONA

SCIENTIFIC NAME: *Panicum torridum*
FAMILY: Graminaceae (also called Poaceae)

Endemic

Kākonakona is another pretty, silky-soft, and "pettable" bunch grass. It has velvety leaves that enclose the flower and seed stalks.

Some grasses will "bite you" if you touch them the wrong way. They have irritating hairs, thorns, and spines. Ask hikers how they like going past alien palm grass while wearing shorts. Ask a *keiki* who tried to walk barefoot across Kapi'olani Park and got stuck by sandburs.

This native grass begs to be petted and pampered and planted in our gardens.

$\mathcal{S}$HRUBS

There are many attractive native Hawaiian shrubs or bushes that can be used in the landscape. They can be used as specimen plants, massed to make a hedge or windbreak, planted thickly for ground cover, or grown in pots to grace your garden or lanai. Some shrubs, such as *'a'ali'i* and *naio*, will grow into small trees with time and good growing conditions.

MA'O HAU HELE, ROCK'S KAUA'I HIBISCUS
SCIENTIFIC NAME: *Hibiscus rockii* (syn: *H. calyphyllus*)
FAMILY: Malvaceae (mallow family)

Endemic (some taxonomists think this is a naturalized species; see arguments below)

Hibiscus rockii is a low sprawling shrub with large yellow blossoms. The yellow native hibiscus was selected as the state flower in 1988 because a variety is native to each of the main islands. *Hibiscus rockii* is the variety native to Kaua'i. Its natural growth habit is shrublike: from 2 to 4 feet tall. It is sometimes found in old kamaaina gardens on Kaua'i and the other islands. For some scientists, this is evidence that it is a naturalized species. However, we grew the Kaua'i plant next to the African *H. calyphyllus* in the Honolulu Botanical Gardens, and we found them to be distinct and different. The Kaua'i variety is much prettier, with larger flowers, a more manageable growth habit, and fewer prickles on the base of the flower and along the leaves.

PROPAGATION AND CARE: This hibiscus is easily and rapidly produced from cuttings. It is one of the easiest native plants to grow. Make cuttings about 4 inches long, strip off most of the leaves, and stick the cuttings in a pot or the ground. Water daily and soon most of the cuttings will root.

    Hibiscus rockii is also quite easy to grow from seeds, but cuttings are faster. Remove the small brown, fuzzy, roughly almond-shaped seeds from the pod and plant them in a pot of clean potting mix.

    As with many native members of the genus *Hibiscus*, plants should not be overfertilized or sucking insects will be attracted to and feed on the lush, nitrogen-rich new growth. Overfertilized plants also grow too luxuriantly and become too top-heavy for the roots to support. If you overfertilize by mistake, take out your pruning shears and lace the plant out, removing about one-third of the branches. Make these into cuttings to grow yourself or to share with friends.

Ma'o hau hele, *or Hibiscus bracken-ridgei, our state flower. This form is from Pu'u Anahulu on Hawai'i Island, collected by Dr. Evangeline Funk before the many fires ravaged the area.*

The Kaua'i yellow hibiscus, *or* ma'o hau hele, *is kept low with weed trimmers at the Wailea Beach Hotel. This plant is tough and versatile as a ground cover, hedge, shrub, specimen, or potted planting. In the foreground is* ma'o *(Hawaiian cotton).*

A planting of Kaua'i native Hibiscus rockii, *growing at a new Hawaiian garden in Makawao, Maui.*

LANDSCAPE USE: *Hibiscus rockii* is attractive and blooms well when maintained at a height of 6 to 12 inches. In the landscape it can be kept low with a string or blade trimmer. This has been done for many years at the Wailea Beach Hotel landscape in Mākena on Maui. The planting is healthy and vigorous, and the large yellow flowers are impressive as they bloom out each morning. This plant is also attractive if allowed to grow more freely as a rambling shrub, sprawling over the ground or attractively draped over large moss rocks, or dangling over and concealing a hollow-tile wall. It makes a nice foundation planting around a house. It can also be trained into a hedge. It will grow well in a large pot. The large clear yellow flowers, with their velvety purple-black throats, make striking splashes of color in the garden.

PESTS: *Hibiscus rockii* has few pests unless overfertilized with high amounts of nitrogen. Overfertilization will also encourage pests like scale to attach themselves to the young growth and stems. If this happens, treat with insecticidal soap and remove by hand, or use a standard insecticide. In the future, restrain yourself from excessive fertilizer use.

KOKI'O KE'OKE'O, HAWAIIAN WHITE HIBISCUS

SCIENTIFIC NAMES: *Hibiscus waimeae, Hibiscus arnottianus, Hibiscus immaculatus*
FAMILY: Malvaceae (hibiscus family)

Endemic

Hibiscus waimeae, *native to Kaua'i, blooms happily in a Makiki garden. It was grafted onto a tough root stock.*

The Hawaiian white native hibiscus have several unique attributes. The main one is that the flowers are fragrant. Usually when you try to smell a hibiscus, all you get is pollen on your nose. The Hawaiian whites have a delicate, subtle fragrance. *Hibiscus waimeae*, the Kaua'i white, has a light pink staminal column and pubescent (hairy) light green leaves. The staminal column of *Hibiscus arnottianus*, the O'ahu white, is magenta and the leaves are glabrous (smooth) and dark green. The Moloka'i white, *H. immaculatus*, has a pure white staminal column and smooth light green leaves. Hibiscus Rice White is an old selection of the Kaua'i native *Hibiscus waimeae*. It is very fragrant, with a lasting blossom, and has been used as a parent for many modern hybrids. Hibiscus Kanani Kea is another natural selection, from a nice *Hibiscus arnottianus* on the Mānoa Cliffs Trail in the Ko'olau mountains of O'ahu. This selection was named by Bob Hirano, horticulturist emeritus for the Lyon Arboretum, where it was long propagated and grown. Each of these Hawaiian white hibiscus is unique and possesses a slightly different fragrance. Their propagation and landscape uses are similar, however, so I grouped them together here.

PROPAGATION AND CARE: The usual propagation method is by cuttings, but hibiscus can also be grown from seeds, grafting and air-layering.

Take tip and stem cuttings, 4 to 6 inches long, treat with a medium-strength rooting hormone like rootoneF or #3 Hormex, plant in a rooting mixture of perlite or perlite and vermiculite in pots or flats, and place under a mist system until they develop roots. Once they have rooted, put them into individual pots, in a medium such as peat moss and perlite, with fertilizer incorporated into the mix.

Growing hibiscus from seeds is relatively fast and easy. But because hibiscus, especially the native Hawaiian whites, hybridize so readily, the offspring may be different from the parents. To get pure seed, hand-pollinate the flowers and then cover with a bag to prevent cross-fertilization. Many great hybrid hibiscus grown in Hawai'i today have the Hawaiian whites as parents. You can raise seeds produced by chance crosses and see what grows, or you can cross-pollinate them on purpose.

Grafting is a good method to use for growing *koki'o ke'oke'o*. Use a tough rootstock and graft the native onto it. Hibiscus are among the easiest plants to graft, and the native whites grow quite well this way. One advantage with grafting is that you get a fairly tall, mature plant from just a small scion cutting.

Air-layering is a pretty good method, especially if a fairly large plant is desired. However, sometimes the root systems obtained this way are not as strong as those produced from seedlings, cuttings, or grafted plants.

LANDSCAPE USE: *Koki'o ke'oke'o* is an excellent plant for the landscape. In wet, cool areas in Hawai'i, it can grow into fairly large trees (30 to 40 feet) with time. The more usual form found in most gardens is a rounded, 3–4-foot shrub. It grows well in the ground, or in a very large container.

Koki'o ke'oke'o can be mass-planted to form a hedge, planted singly as a specimen, or grouped as a mass or screen.

PESTS: *Koki'o ke'oke'o* is sometimes attacked by rose beetles, thrips, and aphids. Stink bugs sometimes cause bud drop. You can spray with Safer's insecticidal soap or with standard garden insecticides. Do not use Diazinon on hibiscus. Avoid overfertilizing, especially with nitrogen, or the plant will become too luxuriant and top-heavy for the roots to support it, and pests are attracted to the succulent growth.

OTHER USES: The early Hawaiians used the buds of *koki'o ke'oke'o* as a mild, pleasant-tasting laxative. One report says that these white flowers were medicine for girl children, while the native red hibiscus, *koki'o 'ula*, was for boys. The fiber was used for cordage and tying.

Hibiscus saintjohnianus, *from the Nā Pali Coast of Kaua'i, is a yellow-orange or red hibiscus with a unique shape.*

The fragrant white Hibiscus immaculatus *almost became extinct as a result of the ravages of feral goats, pigs, and deer in its rain forest home on the north side of Moloka'i. Horticulturists led by Keith Wooliams of Waimea Botanical Garden found a surviving plant clinging desperately to life on a dry slope where the animals couldn't eat it, and brought it into cultivation. It grows well in Hawai'i gardens.*

KO'OLOA 'ULA, "RED" 'ILIMA

SCIENTIFIC NAME: *Abutilon menziesii*
FAMILY: Malvaceae (hibiscus family)

Endemic

Ko'oloa 'ula is a shrub with silvery, heart-shaped leaves and small, pendent (hanging) red blossoms. It is related to hibiscus and *'ilima*. This shrub grows from 3 to 6 feet tall. It has a somewhat straggly growth habit in the wild but can be pruned into a more attractive shape. *Ko'oloa 'ula* is a federally listed endangered species. It is so rare in the wild because its habitat has been destroyed by development, weeds, introduced animals and diseases.

PROPAGATION AND CARE: *Ko'oloa 'ula* can be grown from cuttings, air-layers, or seeds. Planting seeds is the easiest method for producing new plants.

LANDSCAPE USE: This shrub can be trained in an arborescent form or kept as a smaller shrub. It makes an interesting specimen and would also be attractive as a hedge. It is very tough and drought tolerant. The pendent red flowers are a surprise and delight to gardeners.

PESTS: *Ko'oloa 'ula* is sometimes attacked by chewing and sucking insects. These are controlled with standard garden insecticides in wettable powder formulations or with regular sprays of insecticidal soap. You can also plant near a streetlight to repel rose beetles.

OTHER USES: If you can get enough flowers, they can be fashioned into a striking lei.

'A'ALI'I

SCIENTIFIC NAME: *Dodonaea viscosa*
FAMILY: Sapindaceae (lychee family)

Indigenous to Hawai'i and across the tropics

'A'ali'i is a shrub, or with time a small tree. It ranges from 3 to 10 feet in height. The leaves are glossy green with reddish midribs and stems. The flowers are either male or female and are fairly small and insignificant (about 1/4 inch in diameter). The female flowers develop into attractive, papery fruit capsules. These capsules come in a variety of colors: red, pink, green, yellow, and tan. The male flowers are tiny, about 1/4 inch wide, red, yellow, or green, and shaped like a curled-up octopus. They produce abundant pollen, which is blown or carried by insects to the female flowers. *'A'ali'i* is one of those Hawaiian plants with a very broad natural range. It can be found in coastal areas like Polihale on Kaua'i and Koko Head on O'ahu, but it ranges up to high, dry sites like Haleakalā and the Volcano area on the Big Island.

In this close-up it is easy to see that ko'oloa 'ula *is* related to hibiscus and 'ilima. Ko'oloa 'ula *is easy to grow and makes an unusual and striking lei.*

A'ali'i's *female flowers have a pistil protruding from the center and start out looking like a miniature of the fruit they will develop into.*

A Hawaiian proverb says a lot about the characteristics of 'a'ali'i: "He 'a'ali'i kū makani mai au; 'a'ohe makani nāna e kula'i" (I am the wind-resisting 'a'ali'i; no gale can push me over). In other words, "I can hold my own even in the face of difficulties." The 'a'ali'i bush can stand the worst of gales, twisting and bending but seldom breaking off or falling over.

'A'ali'i is a tough, wind- and drought-resistant plant. It has a strong and fibrous root system. It is a great plant for many different types of Hawaiian garden. It is also a plant that will grow well in a large pot on the lanai of your apartment or rented house.

The 'a'ali'i that grows on the rugged slopes of Hualālai is a deep burgundy color, possibly as a result of the harsh and changing conditions on this high and usually dry mountain.

PROPAGATION AND CARE: 'A'ali'i is best grown from seeds. Soaking the seeds for 24 hours in water that initially was boiling hot will improve and speed up germination of the tiny hard seeds. These round black seeds are found inside the papery capsules. You can sometimes gently take apart an old *lei haku* and grow the seeds within. Plant the presoaked seeds in a pot of clean, well-drained potting mix. Water daily; the seeds will sprout in two weeks to a month. When they have two sets of leaves, transplant them into individual small pots. Move them into larger pots as they grow. They can be put into the ground or into permanent large pots when they are from 6 inches to 2 feet tall.

'A'ali'i has a broad elevation range and is not particular as to soil type, as long as it is well drained. You can also grow 'a'ali'i from cuttings or air-layers.

LANDSCAPE USE: In the landscape, 'a'ali'i is useful as a specimen shrub, hedge material, or tree. It responds well to pruning. Given full sun and good drainage, 'a'ali'i should thrive in any Hawai'i garden.

If your garden has a claylike or other slow-draining soil, there are several remedies. You can mix in coarse volcanic cinders or perlite; you can create a mound or utilize one that is already present; or you can plant on a slope. Planting along a stone or hollow-tile wall also helps to provide good drainage.

PESTS: 'A'ali'i has few pests. Once in a while (especially if you fertilize with too much nitrogen), scale insects attach themselves to the stems and new leaves and suck sap. Don't overfertilize, and treat the scale with garden insecticides or insecticidal soap, or scrape them off with a fingernail or old toothbrush.

OTHER USES: The seed capsules are attractive and are prized for *lei haku*. They are also nice as a "flower" in your hair. Flower arrangers have recently discovered them and use them in dry and fresh arrangements. If hung to dry in a well-ventilated area, the fruit clusters will keep for years. A red-yellow kapa dye was produced from 'a'ali'i. The tough, hard wood was used for house poles, spears, and 'ō'ō (digging sticks).

Beautiful 'a'ali'i grows beside dry grasses on the Big Island, near Waimea. The highly flammable grasses spread wildfires that devastate 'a'ali'i and other natives. The weedy fountain grass is fire adapted and comes right back after incineration.

Ma'o thrives in this dry, rocky area at Ka Iwi, or Queen's Beach, O'ahu. However, off-road vehicles scrambling in the area and fires started by careless smokers threaten its future.

This bright yellow ma'o *flower is so perfect it almost looks artificial. The early Hawaiians made green dye from* ma'o.

Shrub form of ma'o, *or Hawaiian cotton, growing at Wailea, Maui*

MA'O, HAWAIIAN COTTON

SCIENTIFIC NAME: *Gossypium tomentosum*
FAMILY: Malvaceae (hibiscus family)

Endemic

Ma'o is a shrub 3 to 6 feet tall and equally wide. It has silvery-green leaves shaped like *kukui* or maple leaves, clear yellow flowers 2 to 3 inches in diameter, and seed capsules that hold fuzzy brown seeds with short cottonlike hairs.

PROPAGATION AND CARE: *Ma'o* is readily propagated from seeds. A 24-hour hot water soak improves germination. *Ma'o* can also be grown from cuttings and air-layers.

LANDSCAPE USE: *Ma'o* is attractive if grown naturally or pruned and shaped. It can be used as a specimen shrub or a hedge. It does well in a large pot on a sunny lanai.

PESTS: *Ma'o* does have some pest problems from chewing and sucking insects and from nematodes. Use standard wettable powder insecticides for the former. Nematodes can be restrained by using Clandosan, incorporated with fertilizer and other amendments at the time of planting. Clandosan is a natural by-product of the shellfish industry. The chitin contained in it is food for beneficial organisms that eat nematode eggs.

OTHER USES: Although *ma'o* is not useful for textile production, it has been used by plant breeders to improve the pest resistance of commercial cotton. The early Hawaiians made a green dye for kapa from *ma'o*. Modern kapa makers have tried to reproduce this gorgeous yet subtle green dye and have so far been unsuccessful—they don't know what the missing ingredient or dying technique was. The Hawaiian word for green is *'ōma'oma'o*. *Ho'ōma'oma'o* means to make or paint green.

KO'OKO'OLAU

SCIENTIFIC NAME: *Bidens* spp.
FAMILY: Asteraceae (sunflower family)

Endemic (19 species)

Ko'oko'olau is the Hawaiian name for a large group of endemic plants, all members of the genus *Bidens*. These plants are bushes or shrubs, but sometimes they grow to tree size, and there is even a vinelike species. *Ko'oko'olau* has bright yellow, flat daisylike flowers. The different species and forms are native to the different islands, and sometimes to certain areas of each island.

There is also a weedy type of non-native *Bidens* called beggar's tick or Spanish needle, often seen in Hawai'i. If you look at the seeds of this weed and compare them to seeds of most of the native species, you can see a point in Hawaiian evolution. The alien seed has two barbs on its end. These barbs attach the seeds to your clothes, your backpack, and to dogs and other animals, and in this way the weed seeds are spread all over. The Hawaiian plants typically don't have these barbed seeds, because people and animals like dogs and pigs were not here to carry them around when they evolved. Instead, the Hawaiian seeds are curved and twisty so they can roll down a hill and find new places to grow, with the help of passing gusty Hawaiian breezes.

Ko'oko'olau flowers are a mass of yellow. *Grow this plant as you would its common cousin the marigold.*

PROPAGATION AND CARE: *Ko'oko'olau* is pretty easy to grow. Treat it like a flowering marigold (another member of this family). Water and fertilize regularly, pinch the tips off for tea and to make the plants bushier. Plants can be grown from seeds or cuttings.

Ko'oko'olau is not always offered for sale at your local nursery, but as a good consumer advocate for native Hawaiian plants you should always inquire and encourage more to be grown. Sometimes botanical gardens such as Wahiawa, Waimea or Lyon Arboretum offer native plants for sale.

Once you get a plant or two, you can easily grow more to share and perpetuate this native Hawaiian plant. Grow more from small cuttings or fresh, ripe seeds that you can collect from your mother plants.

LANDSCAPE USE: *Ko'oko'olau* can be an attractive blooming shrub for your landscape. It sometimes is not long-lived, so think of it as an annual marigold that you have to pinch back for lots of flowers and compact growth, and periodically replant it from new plants grown directly from seeds sown in the ground or from potted plants grown from seeds or cuttings.

PESTS: *Ko'oko'olau* will get sucking insect pests like aphids and scales if you use too much nitrogen-rich fertilizer. Have a light hand with the nitrogen, and if your plants do get infested, remove the pests by hand, smash them, and treat the plant with insecticidal soap.

Note the barbless seeds on this native ko'oko'olau. *This is one of the main things that distinguish the natives from the alien introduction.*

OTHER USES: At a meeting of the Ladies of the Royal Order of Kamehameha, the topic was water. Kupuna Elizabeth Nālani Ellis spoke of her girlhood on the Hāmākua coast: "We had to all hike up to the spring with water buckets before and after school to get water for our grandmother to do all the daily tasks. Our spring was very clean and good and always kept running because our tutu would have us clean it out just so. We ate lots of poi and taro. Whenever we wanted to drink tea it would be *ko'oko'olau*, but I've never seen what the [live, blooming] plant looks like until tonight. [We had watched slides of native Hawaiian plants earlier in the evening.] My father would go up in 'the Bush,' as we called it. He'd bring back a big branch, dry it by hanging it on the wall, and we'd have a big bag of the dried leaves and flowers. Whenever we wanted tea, we grabbed a handful of *ko'oko'olau* and brewed it up. I didn't much like the taste at the time."

When she told us this story, she was 93 years old. She had all her own teeth and only one filling. Her skin was to die for and her mind . . . so *akamai*. She was living proof that this prescription works: hard work, taro, pure Hawaiian water, and *ko'oko'olau* tea.

The early Hawaiians also drank *ko'oko'olau* as a tea. You can gather the leafy and flowering tips and brew them fresh, but after they have dried they work, too. This drink is said to lower high blood pressure and relieve stomach distress. I have been making tea for my dad's blood pressure. The doctor gives him pills, but he gets so riled every time he has to go see the doctor that the pills don't seem to do the trick as well as *ko'oko'olau* tea from the backyard. We have all been drinking it, because it has a good flavor and we could all use a complexion like Kupuna Nālani Ellis's.

KULU'Ī

SCIENTIFIC NAME: *Nototrichium sandwicense*
FAMILY: Amaranthaceae (*kulu'ī* family)

Endemic

Kulu'ī is a shrub 3 to 6 feet tall with silvery leaves 2 to 5 inches long and about half as wide. It rarely flowers, and the flowers are insignificant. It is related to *'ewa hinahina* (*Acharanthes splendens*) and ornamental cockscomb. It is native to the dry slopes above Ka'ena Point on O'ahu.

PROPAGATION AND CARE: *Kulu'ī* is easy to grow from cuttings. Collect cuttings and propagate right away. Trim back three-fourths of the leaves, either cutting them off or cutting them in half. Stick several cuttings in a pot of perlite or equal parts perlite and vermiculite. They will also root in a pot of well-drained soil.

LANDSCAPE USE: *Kulu'ī* is naturally a large shrub. It can be allowed to grow in its natural shape or pruned and shaped to suit a particular landscape. *Kulu'ī* will also grow in a large clay or cement pot on a sunny lanai.

Kulu'ī has not been used much yet in Hawaiian landscapes, but we should be seeing more of it in the future as landscape architects, contractors, and home gardeners discover this tough and good-looking native Hawaiian shrub. There are a few places where you can see it and get inspired. At Kahua Lehua in Ho'omaluhia Botanical Garden, there is a mass planting of *kulu'ī* growing on a sunny slope. It looks great and has been growing there since the mid 1980s. A new planting utilizing *kulu'ī*, designed by innovative landscape architect Lester Inouye, is at the Oceanic Institute in Waimānalo. As you drive along Kalaniana'ole Highway, just past Makapu'u, look at the silvery hedge growing above the stone wall. The plants look good, and they stand up well to the almost continuous salty wind hitting them. These plants were installed just before Hurricane 'Iniki, and they took a beating when they were

Kulu'ī leaves become greener and larger the more you water and fertilize. If you would like the plant to be more silvery, you can limit the amount of water it receives.

young and vulnerable, but they are thriving now. The National Tropical Botanical Garden on Kaua'i took a severe beating from 'Iniki. But it is recovering nicely, and so are its native plantings, including *kulu'i*.

PESTS: *Kulu'i* has few pests.

OTHER USES: *Kulu'i* leaves can be made into an attractive silvery *"maile"* lei. Flower arrangers who work with fresh or dry plant materials should grow *kulu'i* and try it in their arrangements.

NAIO, BASTARD SANDALWOOD

SCIENTIFIC NAME: *Myoporum sandwicense*
FAMILY: Myoporaceae (*naio* family)

Indigenous to Hawai'i and to Mangaia in the Cook Islands

Naio is a large shrub or small tree, ranging from 3 to 15 feet high. It has either glossy green or waxy pointed leaves and small flowers clustered close to the stem. The flowers are either pink or white, depending on the variety. The fruit is white and glossy when it is fresh, and shrivels and turns brown with age. *Naio* has a very large natural range, from coastal strand areas to high dry sites in the Hawaiian highlands. It also has family relatives in eastern Asia and through most of the Pacific. In New Zealand it is called *ngaio*.

Naio grows in shrub form at Wailea, Maui. Note Kaho'olawe in the background.

PROPAGATION AND CARE: *Naio* can be grown from seeds or cuttings. Collect the fresh seeds found inside the white fruit and clean off the pulp before sowing. The seeds, like those of several plants of Hawaiian dryland areas, sprout sporadically. This may be a survival mechanism of the *naio* plant. Seedlings might die if seeds sprouted when the weather was too hot and dry or too cold and wet. By germinating over a longer period of time, some of the keiki plants are bound to survive. Cuttings should be 3 to 5 inches long. Use rooting hormones, and water or mist regularly to encourage them to root.

 Naio is somewhat slow-growing in the initial stages. It can be pruned, but this must be done with caution, since it does not flush out rapidly. The plants should be in a vigorous state of growth when pruning and shaping are performed.

LANDSCAPE USE: *Naio* has a broad natural elevational range. It grows well on beach areas and sand dunes close to pounding waves, in places like Ka'ena point on O'ahu, the dry Mākena side of Maui, and Polihale on Kaua'i. It lives in the Hawaiian dry forest, in places like Kānepu'u on Lāna'i and Auwahi on Maui, and it grows way up the slopes of drier sides of Mauna Kea and Haleakalā. *Naio* is still found at 10,000 feet on Mauna Kea. This vast natural range of dry climates translates well in the garden. *Naio* can grow well in just about any

To plant naio *from seeds, remove the pulp from the fresh white fruit, soak the seeds in water, and plant them in a clean pot of well-drained medium. Water daily.*

'A'ali'i *and* naio *grow at Kanepu'u, Lāna'i, as very wind-, drought-, and erosion-proof native plants. This photo shows how well they can grow in the toughest conditions, if given some nurturing and protection.*

It is easy to grow new naupaka *plants from fruit or cuttings.*

Hawaiian garden, provided that it has three basic ingredients: sun, well-drained soil, and enough watering to get established. *Naio* is an excellent choice for the xeriscape garden. Although *naio* is usually a large shrub or small tree, one 70 feet tall was recorded in north Kona. *Naio* has either glossy green or waxy pointed leaves and small flowers clustered close to the stem. The flowers are either pink or white, depending on the variety. Fruit follows the flowers.

   Naio is a good specimen or hedge plant. Its broad natural range indicates that it will do well in coastal as well as upland sites in Hawai'i. It is very tough and drought-tolerant in the landscape. It can be grown in a large pot on a sunny lanai.

PESTS: *Naio* has few pests or disease problems. Scale and greenhouse orthusia sometimes attach themselves to the new stem growth. Pick them off by hand and smash them, or treat with insecticidal soap or standard insecticide.

OTHER USES: *Naio* becomes woody with time. The wood has a sandalwood-like fragrance when freshly cut, but eventually it loses its fragrance. Some of the first loads of sandalwood sent to China in the late eighteenth century had a lot of *naio* wood mixed in. By the time the shipment reached China, little scent was left in the *naio* wood, and some loads were rejected by the Chinese traders.

   Naio has relatively hard wood, and it burns well and long with a clear light. It was one of the woods preferred by early Hawaiians for building construction. Because of its long-burning quality, it was also used to make torches for night fishing. It is also a strong and durable wood for woodworking. The Hawaiians had a special name for *naio* wood, especially that from old or dead trees: *'a'aka.*

NAUPAKA KAHAKAI, BEACH NAUPAKA

SCIENTIFIC NAME: *Scaevola sericea*
FAMILY: Goodeniaceae (*naupaka* family)

Indigenous to Hawai'i and other tropic and subtropical Pacific and Indian Ocean coasts

Naupaka kahakai (the *naupaka* by the sea, or beach *naupaka*), is a shrub often grown as a hedge or in a mass of plants. It has large, paddle-shaped light green leaves that are fairly succulent. White, fragrant half-flowers are found nestled among the leaves. The flowers are followed by white berries. The seeds inside the berries are beige, corky, and ridged.

   Naupaka is indigenous to much of the Pacific: the same beach species is a native here in Hawai'i and also in other places throughout Polynesia. By contrast, another member of this genus, *S. procera, naupaka kuahiwi* (mountain *naupaka*), is endemic, or unique, to Hawai'i. This plant reached Hawai'i on a "different trip" than beach *naupaka. Naupaka kuahiwi* has a berrylike fruit that is often purple, and it probably came to Hawai'i on or inside birds. Today, its flowers are pollinated by native Hawaiian birds, and the seeds are spread by birds eating them and then making kukai with the seeds inside.

Although the voyaging methods of many native plants are in question, it is pretty clear how *naupaka kahakai* managed to travel to the Hawaiian Islands. The white, fleshy fruit is buoyant and can float for years. The tiny *keiki* plant or embryo of the seed can tolerate salt water, too, and remains alive for years. In this regard, *naupaka* is unlike the *niu* (coconut), which had to be carried here in the voyaging canoes of the ancient Polynesians. We all know that coconuts too can float in the ocean, but with time the nut becomes waterlogged, and the *keiki* or embryo cannot live for a long time in salt water. *Niu* could float between the close islands of an archipelago, as in Tahiti, the Marquesas, or Sāmoa, and sprout when it reached its new home. But the Hawaiian Islands are the most isolated high islands in the world. The vast Pacific, plus ocean currents veering away from Hawai'i, make for a long, tough journey. With time and luck, some coconuts and *naupaka* seeds could wash up here. The *naupaka* would probably grow; the coconut wouldn't.

Though this seems like common sense, and scientists talk about it, it took a young Hawai'i student to prove it. Dianella Howarth loves and wanted to study animals. But our native animals are few and far between nowadays, and so they are hard for an intermediate school student to study. Rain forest birds and insects are, well, in the rain forests and are rare and hard to see. The native Hawaiian bat, *ōpe'ape'a*, is extremely rare. Until recent years you could hardly see a Hawaiian monk seal here in the main islands, and of course fish and *'opihi*-type animals are in the ocean. So Dianella decided to study a native Hawaiian plant, the *naupaka*.

She did some fairly simple experiments that take a long time. She found that *naupaka kahakai* germinated best after a 250-day soak in salt water. Although it will sprout right off the bush, it will also grow after a long saltwater soak. Dianella is continuing her experiments to see how many years beach *naupaka* can soak in salt water and still grow.

Naupaka kahakai is perfectly adapted to the hot, dry lowlands of Hawai'i. It has thick succulent leaves to conserve moisture in dry times. It loves ocean spray. It can take strong, drying winds. Some of the most beautiful *naupaka kahakai* plants grow in the harshest Hawaiian places, like Ka'ena point on O'ahu, bone-dry Mākena on Maui, or windy Lōpā on Lāna'i. Once established in the ground, it can drink salt water—but as with all of us, a drink of precious fresh Hawaiian water is beneficial for *naupaka* as well.

PROPAGATION AND CARE: *Naupaka kahakai* is easy to grow. Even if you say you have a "brown or black thumb," *naupaka* is one native Hawaiian plant you can probably manage to grow. The seeds will sprout easily, even without that 250-day saltwater soak. You can also make slips or cuttings from the branches and grow new plants.

This *naupaka* is growing at Ka'ena Point on the Wai'anae coast, O'ahu. Years of motorbike and off-road vehicle traffic have left this shattered pattern of growth. When plants are protected from vehicles, naupaka is the first to recover and provides shelter for other smaller and more vulnerable plants. In your garden, start with naupaka for sheltering and windbreaking and plant your other plants around the naupaka.

Naupaka kuahiwi, or *mountain naupaka, growing naturally at Ho'omaluhia Botanical Garden. The half flowers are the inspiration for several romantic Hawaiian legends.*

Even a fairly big branch (up to 3 feet long) can be cut off the mother plant and stuck in the ground or a pot. Cut some of the leaves off, so that not too much moisture is lost from the new plant. Water your seeds or new cuttings daily, and they should grow. If a large specimen plant is desired it can be propagated by air-layering.

LANDSCAPE USE: *Naupaka kahakai* makes a great windbreak. It can also provide a hedge for your yard and can be used to shelter other more vulnerable native plants. It does great near the beach and also grows well inland and up mauka. Like many coastal Hawaiian plants, it can thrive in upland gardens if you give it full sun and well-drained soil.

PESTS: There are few pests or diseases associated with beach naupaka.

OTHER USES: The leaves are used regularly by snorkelers and divers to defog their face masks. Before they enter the water, they break a leaf in half and smear the sap on the inside of the glass.

There is a famous Hawaiian legend about *naupaka kahakai*. In the olden days, all *naupaka* had complete flowers. There were two young lovers who couldn't be together for one reason or another (some say Pele was in love with the man, others say their parents didn't approve of the match). One day, after the lovers tried to hide together, the woman lost her patience. She plucked a *naupaka* blossom, tore it in half, gave one half to her lover, and fled with the other half. The gods took pity on the lovers and turned them each into a plant with half-flowers, one the beach *naupaka* and one the mountain *naupaka*—and so all *naupaka* have half-flowers to this day. If you find one with a whole flower, we can rejoice—it means the lovers finally got together.

Naupaka kahakai *flowers are mildly fragrant. The leaves of this coastal plant are good for defogging diving goggles.*

MĀMAKI

SCIENTIFIC NAME: *Pipturis albidus*
FAMILY: Urticaceae (nettle family)

Endemic

Māmaki was here in the Islands growing and evolving with the other forms of life around it long before people ever pulled up onto the beaches of Hawai'i, and it is a native nowhere else in the world. You can see it along many trails in Hawai'i and in botanical gardens. I have a large one in my yard that screens an objectionable view and muffles noise. *Māmaki* can be seen along the Mānoa Cliffs Trail in the Ko'olaus and along the Honouliuli Contour Trail in the Wai'anaes. Wahiawa Botanical Garden has several large plants, as does Lyon Arboretum in Mānoa.

Māmaki has large, light-green leaves with prominent veins that may be green, pink, or red. Edible white berries come out along the leaf branches and are full of tiny seeds. In the wild they are eaten and spread by native Hawaiian birds.

There are many ways that we can tell that *māmaki* is an ancient resident. It is food for the larvae of our rare native Kamehameha *pulelehua*, the butterfly. The larvae feed on *māmaki* leaves and the leaves of other native nettles.

In other parts of the world, members of the Urticaceae family include stinging nettles, plants that look like *māmaki* but have stinging hairs. You know when you have brushed against one—it feels like a wasp sting and raises a painful welt. When I was working at the Royal Horticultural Society's garden at Wisley in England, I hated nettles. I would brush against them as I rode my push bike to work, or they would zap me as I weeded them. In my youthful horticultural vigor, I wanted to exterminate them from the English countryside. Fortunately, one of the naturalists at the garden set me straight: "But Heidi, you silly Hawaiian girl, seven species of endemic English butterflies have larvae that feed exclusively on stinging nettles!"

Māmaki leaves are highlighted by attractive red, pink, or light-green veins. These large leaves are edible and medicinal and are the food for our *pulelehua, the Kamehameha butterfly.*

PROPAGATION AND CARE: *Māmaki* can be grown from seeds or cuttings. Separate the tiny seeds from the pulp in water and sow on fine, moist, well-compacted potting medium. Water regularly. Cuttings 4 to 6 inches long will grow fairly readily. It is an easy plant to grow in mauka gardens; lowland gardeners will have to struggle more to make it thrive.

LANDSCAPE USE: *Māmaki* is very attractive and has many uses. Its being the food of a vanishing Hawaiian butterfly is another reason to grow it, especially if you live near a forested area.

PESTS: *Māmaki* has few pests.

OTHER USES: Our *māmaki* didn't need to defend itself against people and animals in the olden days before humans found Hawai'i. You can eat the leaves raw or cooked. In other parts of the world, thoroughly cooked stinging nettles are a nutritious dark green leafy vegetable. Our Hawaiian variety is even better.

Some reports state that the early Hawaiians made a type of kapa from *māmaki*. Evangaline Funk, who studied Hawaiian fiber plants, doubts this claim. She found that *māmaki* fibers are too short to make useful kapa. *Wauke*, the paper mulberry brought by the Polynesians to Hawai'i, made the best kapa.

Māmaki was also used medicinally by the ancient Hawaiians, and many people use it today. It is usually made into a delicious tea.

MA'O HAU HELE

SCIENTIFIC NAME: *Hibiscus brackenridgei*
FAMILY: Malvaceae (hibiscus family)

Endemic

Ma'o hau hele is a shrub 4 to 8 feet tall with large clear yellow flowers. It blooms most profusely in spring and early summer. The flowers are

O'ahu ma'o hau hele, *our state flower, is native to the Wai'anae Mountains.*

Abutilon eremitopetalum, *the hidden-petaled 'ilima, was until recently thought to be extinct. On Lāna'i, alien axis deer had munched it, rubbed it with their antlers, and nearly stomped it to death. When the plants are fenced to keep deer away, they are easy to grow. Photo by Dr. Diane Ragone, courtesy of the National Tropical Botanical Garden.*

from 4 to 6 inches in diameter. There is a form or variety native to each of the main Hawaiian islands. *Ma'o hau hele* is Hawai'i's official state flower. It was designated so by the 1988 Legislature. Interestingly, Dr. William Hillebrand, the initial planter of Foster Botanical Garden, suggested in 1888 that *ma'o hau hele* be given some kind of official recognition, since it has such showy, bright yellow blossoms.

PROPAGATION AND CARE: *Ma'o hau hele* can be most easily grown from cuttings. Seeds also work well but are slower.

LANDSCAPE USE: *Ma'o hau hele* responds well to pruning and shaping, especially after its main blooming cycle. It is attractive as a specimen shrub, mass planting, or hedge. *Ma'o hau hele* is not a long-lived plant in the wild, dying after four to six years. It can be maintained longer in cultivation with proper care (pruning, fertilizing, and watering), but it is a good idea to rejuvenate the planting after about five years.

PESTS: Chewing and sucking insects sometimes attack *ma'o hau hele*. Spray with standard wettable powder insecticides or Safer's insecticidal soap.

HIDDEN-PETALED *'ILIMA*

SCIENTIFIC NAME: *Abutilon eremitopetalum*
FAMILY: Malvaceae (hibiscus family)

Endemic

The hidden-petaled *'ilima* has fuzzy, heart-shaped leaves and small, pendant (hanging) flowers. The flowers have no true petals, just a green calyx and a protruding orange-yellow staminal column.

Abutilon eremitopetalum was thought to be extinct; it had not been seen since the 1920s. Steve Perlman, of Hawai'i Tropical Botanical Garden, rediscovered it while looking for it and other rare plants on Lāna'i. He found a few plants "eaten to the six-foot level by alien axis deer." He collected seeds and shared them with different botanical gardens and Hawaiian plant growers, and we found that they are very easy to grow.

PROPAGATION AND CARE: The hidden-petaled *'ilima* grows readily from seeds.

LANDSCAPE USE: This plant makes an interesting specimen or shrub plant. Like many native members of the hibiscus family, it should be pruned to keep it from getting too top-heavy. Sometimes fertilizer makes the top growth too heavy and luxuriant for the roots to support.

PESTS: Few pests are recorded for this plant.

HAU KUAHIWI

SCIENTIFIC NAME: *Hibiscadelphus distans, H. hualalaiensis*
FAMILY: Malvaceae (hibiscus family)

Endemic genus

Hau kuahiwi has curved, tubular flowers, perfect for the curved beak of a Hawaiian honeycreeper to sip nectar from and pollinate. The whole genus is endemic to Hawai'i—found only here and co-evolved with native forest birds. The leaves are somewhat silvery. It is a rare plant that is fairly easy to grow in the garden. It is related to hibiscus.

PROPAGATION AND CARE: Grow *hau kuahiwi* from seeds. Provide rich, well-drained soil and water regularly. Keep notes about the growing and horticulture (what seems to work and what doesn't), to add to our horticultural knowledge.

LANDSCAPE USE: *Hau kuahiwi* is usually a bush or shrub in the garden. With time and optimum growing conditions it may become a small tree. We need to grow and test this plant more under garden conditions, as well as protect the few remaining trees in the wild.

Some are growing well at the Honolulu Zoo, under the expert care of reptile specialist Jamison Martinez. They thrive at Waimea Arboretum. You can also see them growing semiwild at Kīpukapuaulu near Hawai'i Volcanoes National Park.

PESTS: *Hau kuahiwi* is highly endangered in the wild. It may be attacked by the usual garden pests: sucking and chewing insects, twig borers, etc. Keep a close eye on your plants; use a light hand with fertilizer and use gentle pest controls like insecticidal soap and hand picking. Systemic granular insecticides like Merit and Marathon can provide preventive insect control for truly nasty and insidious pests like twig borers.

OTHER USES: Growing *hau kuahiwi* may attract native Hawaiian birds to your garden, especially if you are near an intact Hawaiian forest. This plant is a prime candidate for horticultural salvation.

PUA PILO, MAIAPILO, PILO, NATIVE CAPER

SCIENTIFIC NAME: *Capparis sandwichiana*
FAMILY: Capparidaceae (also called Capparaceae) (caper family)

Indigenous

Pua pilo has an amazingly beautiful and unique fragrant white evening-blooming blossom with multiple feathery stamens and 4 bright white petals that are about 2 inches long. You can find freshly opened blossoms in the evening and early morning. By hot mid morning the flowers have faded and become tinged with purple. If

Hau kuahiwi, *with a curved, tubular flower filled with sweet nectar, is bird pollinated. Hawaiian naturalists believe that* hau kuahiwi *flowers coevolved with curved-beak nectar-feeding Hawaiian honeycreepers and other native birds.*

Pua pilo *displays its striking, fragrant flowers at dusk. Early in the morning the flowers are still fresh, but as the sun hits, they wilt, take on purple tints, and fade by the next sunset. Photo by Liz Huppman.*

Can you find the green fruit of the pua pilo, *our native Hawaiian caper? On Oʻahu, ripe fruit is rare because alien bulbuls eat it when it's still green. The plants are becoming rare in the wild. Photo by Liz Huppman.*

Perfectly ripe and collectible fruit of pua pilo. *The orange pulp encases ripe black seeds. In old Hawaiʻi, native birds would have eaten and spread them; today, gardeners need to kōkua this choice Hawaiian plant. Photo by Liz Huppman.*

the plant is pollinated, long, somewhat bumpy green fruits develop. The fruit has 6 ridges and is botanically a berry. There are many small brownish black seeds inside the not-so-ʻono–smelling orange pulp. This once common plant of the coasts and low drylands is becoming rarer, largely as a result bulldozing for development and other land changes.

PROPAGATION AND CARE: *Pua pilo* can be grown from ripe seeds with the pulp cleaned off. It is fairly easy to sprout, but is finicky about soil conditions. In the wild you find it happy on clinkery ʻaʻā lava and in beach sand or sandy soil. In a pot it needs perfect drainage.

LANDSCAPE USE: This plant has great potential in the landscape. As a specimen shrub, as ground cover, in the rock garden, or in the moonlit garden it is most appealing. There are challenges for the grower because it has very specific soil requirements. If you are lucky enough to have land with *pua pilo* on it, leave it alone, treasure it! Once bulldozed, the ʻaʻā lava lands will not resprout *pua pilo*— only weeds will grow in its place.

Pua pilo is very tough and long-lived in the wild and is perfect for the zero-maintenance xeriscape.

PESTS: On Oʻahu alien bulbul birds threaten *pua pilo* since they love to eat the fruit, as a source of vitamin C. We need to protect the developing fruit from these hungry birds. Place a mesh bag around the fruit, or make bird-scaring devices.

Soil fungi may threaten young plants, so make sure to use clean sterile pots and media.

OTHER USES: *Pua pilo* was used as medicine in old Hawaiʻi, for muscle strains, aches, and broken bones. The whole plant was crushed and applied to the joints of the body. *Pua pilo* was not applied directly to the injury. There were probably other medicinal uses, the knowledge of which is possibly lost to us today.

Pua pilo may be edible and ʻono, like the expensive Italian capers at the grocery store. This would be an interesting edible gourmet crop to pursue, once the basic horticulture has been better worked out.

PUA KALA, NATIVE PRICKLY POPPY

SCIENTIFIC NAME: *Argemone glauca*
FAMILY: Papaveraceae

Indigenous

We have a great native Hawaiian poppy, the *pua kala,* or Hawaiian prickly poppy. Recently some Hawaiʻi plant people spotted this or something very similar offered for big bucks on eBay. Amazing! Our Hawaiian plants do have value and we should grow more of them.

Pua kala is a 6-petaled poppy with a deep purple center. The petals are white and somewhat fragile. This is one of a handful of native plants that have prickles and spines on the leaves and stems, and lots of poky protrusions on the seed pods. One theory about thorny native Hawaiian plants is that the thorns and prickles repelled the voracious beaks of a 3-foot-tall flightless goose (now extinct) that once inhabited the lowlands of Hawai'i. The plants can grow to about 4 feet tall (out of reach of those flightless bird beaks?).

Pua kala grows from the dry lowlands to elevations of about 1,000 feet in dry, rocky areas.

Pua kala, *our native Hawaiian prickly poppy, growing on Lāna'i near a new golf course.*

PROPAGATION AND CARE: *Pua kala* is easy to grow from seeds and will self-sow if you give it a good spot in the garden. The seeds are small, black, and round and look like the poppyseeds used in cooking.

Pua kala needs very good drainage and fairly dry conditions after the seedlings or young plants are well established in the ground.

One of the best display plantings of *pua kala* that I have seen is at the Amy Greenwell Botanical Garden in Kona. Next to a house, with lots of concrete rubble in the soil, their patch of *pua kala* thrives and reseeds itself. It gets minimal moisture even in wet-afternoon Kona because it is protected from rainfall by the eaves of the house. This is an interesting horticultural "trick" that can be used in your garden.

LANDSCAPE USE: *Pua kala* is very striking and unusual in the garden. Its bold silvery leaves, bright white flowers, and somewhat unusual appearance make it an interesting addition to the landscape.

As the above example illustrates, you can use *pua kala* in dry, hard-to-water areas of the garden if you water it for a few months after the initial planting in the ground.

With the bright, light-reflecting colors of its flowers and foliage, it is a good addition to the evening garden,

PESTS: *Pua kala* attracts no apparent severe pests, but root fungi and root scales may attack it. It does sometimes die from various "root rots." Keep the soil as sterile as possible (don't import "topsoil"—it never is); well-drained soil and controlled irrigation will help *pua kala* thrive.

Momi Perry with a pua kala *near a silt-protective construction fence. Diligent landscape architect Brenda Lam protected natives during construction of the new golf course on Lāna'i.*

OTHER USES: *Pua kala* has several known medical uses, and there may be more for us to discover. It was used for toothache, ulcers, and neuralgia. There are some narcotic properties in the yellowish sap.

An *'olelo noeau* about *kala*, posed as a riddle and recorded by the late, great Hawaiian linguist Mary Kāwena Pukui, expresses the Hawaiian concept of "*kinolau*," or the different body forms taken on by supernatural beings.

The *kala* of the upland (the *'ākala*: native thornless raspberry)
The *kala* in between (*pua kala*: beach poppy)
The *kala* of the sea (*limu kala*; seaweed)

'ĀNAPANAPA KUKUKU

SCIENTIFIC NAME: *Colubrina asiatica*
FAMILY: Rhamnaceae

Indigenous

'*Ānapanapa* means "glistening," and that's just how the leaf of this native Hawaiian rambling viny shrub looks: glistening in the sun. It can be a medium-sized shrub, or it can grow in a more vinelike way to over 20 feet tall.

This indigenous Hawaiian plant is also native to Africa and India and from Polynesia to Australia. It has several Hawaiian names: *kauila, kauila 'ānapanapa, kauila kukuku,* and, on Ni'ihau, *kolokolo.*

In Hawai'i it is usually found along coastal lowlands, but is becoming less common. A nice clump along the *pali* of Waimea Bay may have been wiped out by all the roadwork there. You certainly can't see it anymore, behind the massive concrete and mesh. It is still fairly common on Moloka'i at Kalaupapa and all along the shoreline on the east end.

'Ānapanapa kukuku *displays its glistening leaves, clusters of small yellow flowers, and ripening fruit on vining branches. The fruits turn brown when ripe and split open to reveal black seeds inside. This is a great plant for riparian (streamside)* 'āina *restoration.*

PROPAGATION AND CARE: '*Ānapanapa* is easy to grow from seeds, especially compared with the much more rare, native upland species of *kauila, Colubrina oppositifolia.* Cuttings and air-layers would probably work as well. It is a tough, less thirsty, wind- and salt-tolerant plant.

Plant it in full sun or partial shade. Well-drained soil is best, but it is a fairly tolerant plant as far as soil goes.

LANDSCAPE USE: You can train '*ānapanapa* as a shrub or ground cover or drape it over a trellis or lanai structure. In the wild it tends to ramble and drape itself over other plants. Take advantage of this growth form as you design your unique landscape.

'*Ānapanapa* is a good choice for the moonlit garden. Its subtle, shiny leaves shimmer and dance the hula to light trade wind breezes under a tropical moon.

PESTS: '*Ānapanapa* attracts no apparent pests, but we need to grow it more in cultivation to find out all of its requirements. As with most natives, good soil preparation, a light hand with fertilizers, and regular monitoring and quick control of pests will help keep '*ānapanapa* healthy and glistening.

OTHER USES: A unique lei is made from '*ānapanapa.* The leaves will lather up in water and are used for soap here in Hawai'i and in Fiji, Samoa, and other places where it grows. In Guam the plant is used medicinally.

KANALOA, PU'U WAI O KANALOA

SCIENTIFIC NAME: *Kanaloa kahoolawensis*
FAMILY: Fabaceae

Endemic

Just when you think there is nothing new under the sun, that every inch of Hawai'i has been botanically surveyed, something new pops up. For years scientists were curious about a mysterious, long gone plant, known only from an ancient pollen signature that they found in deep, old soil deposits from the Salt Lake area on O'ahu. The pollen they found most predominantly was from *loulu* palms, or *Pritchardia*, *'a'ali'i*, or *Dodonaea*, and a mysterious plant that was possibly a legume.

In March 1992, Steve Perlman and Ken Wood, of the National Tropical Botanical Garden, were doing a botanical survey on the goat-and bomb-ravished island of Kaho'olawe. There, on an isolated sea stack in the 'Ale'ale area, on a *pali* inaccessible to the goats, was a strange-looking shrub. Perlman says Wood actually spotted it and they worked together, with skill and strong ropes, to get to the two plants. Perlman precariously perched on the steep, eroding stack, high above the sparkling Pacific. He got a sample and some seeds. The plant was identified as an entirely new genus, a whole group of plants new and unique to scientists. Two plants are growing in the nursery at National Tropical Botanical Garden, clinging perilously to life.

Kanaloa kahoolawensis is the scientific name. *Pu'u wai o Kanaloa* (heart of Kanaloa) is the Hawaiian name, given because of the single heart-shaped seed. There is a *kaona* (double meaning) with Kanaloa, the major Hawaiian god whose special island was Kaho'olawe.

PROPAGATION AND CARE: *Kanaloa* can be grown from seeds, but there are very few to be found. Cuttings and air-layers might work, but the plants are so rare that taking a cutting or putting on an air-layer might send them over the edge. National Tropical Botanical Garden has tried cuttings, grafts, air-layers, and micro propagation, and none of these horticulture techniques have worked, so far.

LANDSCAPE USE: *Kanaloa*, a 3-winged leafed legume, is truthfully not the showiest of plants. It would be interesting to grow for its rarity and educational value, and we should try to grow and nurture these "rarest of the rare" Hawaiian plants.

PESTS: The expert horticulturists at National Tropical Botanical Garden report that *Kanaloa* is a "pest magnet." Every conceivable pest likes to attack it and munch on it. You should definitely check this plant daily and smash or wipe away any pests that try to attack it.

Kanaloa, *from Kaho'olawe, once widespread but now extremely rare, blooms with male flowers only at the Lāwa'i nursery of the National Tropical Botanical Garden. Note the pretty* liko, *or new leaves, of the* kanaloa. *Photo by Nathan Yuen.*

ILIAU

SCIENTIFIC NAME: *Wilkesia gymnoxiphium*
FAMILY: Asteraceae (daisy and sunflower family)

Endemic

Hawai'i has many highly evolved and specialized endemic plants in the daisy family. Possibly, from a single immigrant, a weedy plant called a tarweed that grows in Baja California, evolved silverswords, greenswords, *na'ena'e*, *ko'oko'olau*, and the *iliau* of Kaua'i.

Iliau is found naturally only on Kaua'i. The Iliau Nature Loop, on the way up to Kōke'e State Park on Kaua'i, is one of the few places it grows in abundance. Gardeners have only recently figured out how to grow it.

Like their cousins the silverswords, *iliau* may be monocarpic; that is, the plant flowers once and then dies. The plants don't always do this; some can flower, set seed, and still keep on living and growing. This kind of variability increases the survivorship of the species. *Iliau* usually flower in May and June.

Ricky Cooke at Ho'olana on Moloka'i is growing second-generation *iliau* in his garden. This is a true accomplishment through horticulture. Now that this plant is in cultivation in a garden, seeds don't have to be collected from the wild. There are no native *iliau* on Moloka'i, so growing them at Ho'olana does not harm or otherwise affect the wild populations of *iliau*.

Iliau are also being grown at the Honolulu Zoo in the *nēnē* exhibit. Expert zoo staffers are growing many rare and wonderful Hawaiian plants.

PROPAGATION: Grow *iliau* from seeds. They set thousands of seeds per inflorescence. It is a good plant to grow from seeds and share.

LANDSCAPE USE: *Iliau* is a unique addition to the landscape. It has striking shape and form. Plant *iliau* in a mass. Grow it in a pot, or use it as a specimen. For best growth give it well-drained, cindery soil and full sun.

Iliau, *a Kaua'i native in the sunflower family, is closely related to the silverswords of Haleakalā and Mauna Kea. The inflorescences, silhouetted against the sky, are* pau *blooming and will be full of seeds to grow more* iliau. *Photo by Liz Huppman.*

VINES

Many native Hawaiian vines have great potential for landscape use. An ugly, boring chain-link fence is the ideal place to grow vines such as ʻāwikiwiki. You can construct an arbor or trellis for vines, or you can buy ready-made tomato cages or stakes to support the tendriling growth of your vines. Some will sprawl over and up into trees if you let them. If you have a tough tree or one that you want to cover up, you can plant a Hawaiian vine next to it. The native vine kaunaʻoa is a parasite that can be planted on weeds to suppress them.

Many vine flowers are often used in leis. The handful of vines shared here are lei makers' favorites.

ʻĀWIKIWIKI

SCIENTIFIC NAME: *Canavalia galeata*
FAMILY: Fabaceae (bean family)

Endemic

Some of our most beautiful, rapid-growing but not aggressive vining plants are the ʻāwikiwiki and its other native relatives found on the various islands.

One species of the plant called ʻāwikiwiki by the Hawaiians is native to the Waiʻanae mountains of Oʻahu. It has deep-purple "pea-blossomed" flowers with a splash of magenta, highlighted by several white lines at the throat. It has many native Hawaiian relatives like *wiliwili*, *mamane*, and *koa*. The related flower most of you are familiar with is the lavender-flowered "true *maunaloa*." You may be surprised (like I was) to find out that *maunaloa*, this old-time favorite lei flower with the Hawaiian name, is not native to Hawaiʻi—it was brought in from Madagascar, that large island off the coast of Africa.

PROPAGATION AND CARE: When I first saw an ʻāwikiwiki vine tendriling up the *koa* and sandalwood trees in the Waiʻanaes, I thought, "What a great plant and potential lei flower to try to bring into garden cultivation." My fellow hikers and I looked around and found a few seeds. They are flat, brown, and round or oblong, about 1/2 to 3/4 inches in diameter. They turned out to be easy to grow. Just stick them in the ground where you want them, water regularly, and the seedlings pop up. You can also grow them in a pot for outplanting later, or keep them in a large pot on your sunny lanai.

LANDSCAPE USE: *Āwikiwiki* is happy planted next to a chain-link fence, which it can tendril on and around for support. It flowers beautifully when supported by a fence or even a tough tree like *koa*. You can also let it grow over the ground as a new and different ground cover.

Made in the maunaloa *style, this lei features* ʻāwikiwiki *combined with* palaʻā *fern.*

This is the blossom that inspired bringing ʻawikiwiki *into cultivation. We saw it high up in a tree along the Honouliuli contour trail and thought it would be nice for gardens and lei making. It is an easy vine to grow from seeds.*

PESTS: 'Āwikiwiki's main pest is a black stink bug.

OTHER USES: As I mentioned, *āwikiwiki* makes a great lei. The lei method used to be known as *kui lau* but is now more commonly known as *lei maunaloa*. The flowers are strung crosswise and laid out flat and alternating from each other.

'IE'IE

SCIENTIFIC NAME: *Freycinetia arborea*
FAMILY: Pandanaceae

Indigenous

'Ie'ie, or climbing pandanus, is a woody *liana* of the Hawaiian forest. It has attractive long green leaves with 3 rows of fairly soft spines. You can see the family resemblance to *hala* (pandanus) in the leaf arrangement, the flowers, and the fruits. 'Ie'ie flowers come in sets of 3, and so do the fruits. The fruiting sections look like miniature, elongated *hala* fruits. When the plant prepares to flower, the soft bracts at the center turn orange and the flowers emerge. These bracts are edible.

This was a sacred and revered plant; it is one of the hula plants of Laka and is traditionally placed on the hula altar.

The forked stalks of 'ie'ie somewhat resemble lightning, featured in a legend of how 'ie'ie came to be. There once was a lovely young girl named Lauka'ie'ie (leaf of the 'ie'ie). Hina, the goddess of the moon, cared for Lauka'ie'ie and *hānai*ed her to a lonely couple with no *keiki*. Her playmates in the forest were the birds and the flowers. She fell in love with a bird-man and when the time was right, she married him. It became time for her to change form. Her eyes flashed fire, resembling lightning, and from her sinuous, slender body, long green leaves with 3 precise rows of soft spines sprouted and lengthened as her body stretched and became green. Her husband tenderly carried her and said, "You cannot stand alone anymore; climb trees; twine your supple stems around them. Let your blazing orange flowers shine between the leaves like eyes of fire. Give your beauty to all the *'ōhi'a lehua* trees of the forest." Thus the maiden became the 'ie'ie vine.

The roots were highly prized in old Hawai'i for making an array of fine handcrafted items, including feather helmets and fish traps.

LANDSCAPE USE: You don't see 'ie'ie in the landscape all that much, but the potential is there, especially for *mauka* and rain forest gardens. We grew it up an alien eucalyptus tree at the Wahiawā Botanical Garden for many years, and it is both beautiful and educational.

If you have 'ie'ie on your land, please treasure it and encourage its growth. Propagating plants from your own rain forest laboratory is often the way to find out the secrets to successfully growing native plants.

'Ie'ie *embraces an* 'ōhi'a lehua *along the Mānoa cliffs trail. This is a fairly common plant in wet forests, but we don't know the secrets to growing it widely. There are many cultural uses for the aerial roots, stems, and* lauhala-*like leaves of this climbing hala relative. Photo by Nathan Yuen.*

PROPAGATION: Grow ʻieʻie from seeds or cuttings. It looks like a plant that would be easy to grow ("just stick 'em in like ti leaves" I thought in the early days). I used to collect broken branches of ʻieʻie that trail-clearers and reckless hikers had broken off in passing. None of them grew.

Bob Hobdy and Richard Nakagawa of the Division of Forestry and Wildlife (DOFAW) on Maui told me the ones with lots of young aerial roots on the stalks were the most likely to root out and grow, and that they needed a mist system to grow. I collected some from north Hālawa Valley on Oʻahu as the long-fought H-3 freeway was being constructed through the valley. I collected cuttings that were about 2 feet long with strong, healthy-looking, medium-long aerial roots. (I did this on the advice and with the encouragement of the wise survey archeologist who said the bulldozers would scrape the area bare the next day.) I rushed over to UH-Mānoa and stuck them in the mist system. Two cuttings grew, and one of them was planted onto and supported by a cherry blossom tree in a Wahiawā garden.

Fresh, ripe seeds sprout and become the cutest little mini ʻieʻie, but then often something happens to make all the seedlings damp off, die, and disappear. It may be a fungus or slugs or it may be temperature (too hot in the lowlands) or it may be a combination of several factors. You need to be vigilant when the plants are tiny. They become tough and vigorous later.

You should be able to grow ʻieʻie from air-layers.

PESTS: Mature ʻieʻie have few pests. The seedlings are the vulnerable stage, and slugs, nursery insects, and harmful fungi may attack these. Keep a sharp eye out and use sterile conditions in the nursery to give ʻieʻie a good start in life.

OTHER USES: ʻIeʻie was used for many implements and crafts in old Hawaiʻi. The aerial roots were most prized for making the base of feather helmets, for fine baskets, and for fish and shrimp traps and nets. The roots are strong and pliable and uniformly round. They were used whole or split in half lengthwise.

The leaves are like short, pliable *hala* leaves and were sometimes used for fine plaiting. The leaves around the flowers and fruit are especially fine.

ʻIeʻie is a plant associated with Laka, goddess of hula. It has sacred and ceremonial uses.

KAUNAʻOA

SCIENTIFIC NAME: *Cuscuta sandwichiana*
FAMILY: Cuscutaceae (dodder family)

Endemic

Kaunaʻoa is the lei flower representing the island of Lānaʻi. It does not at first glance look like the most beautiful lei-making plant. But put it in the hands of a skilled lei maker and it is transformed into something beautiful and unique.

ʻIeʻie *flower head displaying abundant pollen. The eye-catching flowers and fruit of* ʻieʻie *are a joy to see in the rain forest or in a home garden.*

This kaunaʻoa *tendrils over* naupaka *at one of the driest places in the world, Polihale, Kauaʻi (also known as Barking Sands).*

Kauna'oa *growing on* pōhuehue, *or beach morning glory, vines on the beach at Kekaha, Kaua'i. This coastal tapestry of colors and textures can be replicated in your own garden.*

From a distance it looks orange-yellow. Up close you can see the different colored strands that are separated and woven into leis. It has small yellow flowers with five petals. The small fruit are capsules with reddish-brown seeds inside.

There are two kinds of *kauna'oa*. One is endemic to Hawai'i and is known as *kauna'oa* or *kauna'oa lei*. This is *Cuscuta sandwichiana*. It is related to *pā'ū-o-Hi'iaka*, *pohuehue*, and other morning glories and is in the Convolvulaceae family. In the old days they called it the "motherless plant" because of its parasitism. "*Kauna'oa* vine, vine of Mana, how I love that orphan vine" is an old proverb that refers to a person who is loved but has no home or family.

The other type is known scientifically as *Cassytha filiformis*; it is native (indigenous) around the world's tropics. It is called *kauna'oa pehu*. The common name is dodder. It is in the avocado or Lauraceae family.

It is hard to tell the two types apart without looking closely at them in a botanical sort of way (examining them under a microscope or hand lens). Both types are good for leis.

Here in Hawai'i *kauna'oa* grows close to the shore and also in the lowland forests. You find it growing on *kiawe* trees, *koa haole*, Christmas berry, and other weedy trees in areas like 'Ewa and Kunia on O'ahu. On Lāna'i it grows beautifully in many places in the dryland forest at Kānepu'u, along the roadsides in the lowlands, and on trees and shrubs along the abandoned pineapple fields. It is particularly beautiful on Hawai'i's beaches.

I had to laugh recently when reading about this mysterious weedy plant in a mainland gardening magazine. They were all wondering how to rid the land of this nasty parasitic weed. "Just make leis out of it and enjoy," I chuckled to my family.

PROPAGATION AND CARE: *Kauna'oa* is a parasitic plant. In the landscape, you can grow it on top of your favorite weeds. Take cuttings of it and wrap them around weeds or other undesirable plants. Smear the seeds on the stems of weeds, or grow *kauna'oa* in a pot that has become infested with weeds. One place to see it growing is the University Avenue cloverleaf off-ramp in Honolulu. A yellow mist seems to cover the weedy grasses that grow there. It has spread to some other off-ramps and wayside areas thanks to the lawn-mowing and weed-trimming equipment used on the areas.

My friend Craig Doyle, expert University Lab School teacher, first showed me how easy *kauna'oa* is to grow. He gathered some from an off-ramp and carried it home to Pālolo, then almost literally flung it into the weeds by his parking space. He now has lei materials close at hand, and his weeds are somewhat suppressed. You too can do this in a weedy or grassy corner of your garden.

LANDSCAPE USE: *Kauna'oa* would be a most unusual plant to grow in a commercial landscape. It would be perfect for any theme lei garden and, of course, is essential for the frequent lei maker's yard. As I mentioned above, growing this plant in your landscape is a creative and certainly pesticide-free way to take care of invading weeds.

Growing Native Hawaiian Plants

PESTS: *Kauna'oa* has few pests.

OTHER USES: The *wili* method of lei making is usually used for *lei kauna'oa*. Two or more strands are woven together. The *kauna'oa* is compared to the *o'o* bird's lovely yellow feathers in the *mele* "Na Lei o Hawai'i."

MAILE

SCIENTIFIC NAME: *Alyxia oliviformis*
FAMILY: Apocynaceae (plumeria family)

Endemic

Hawaiian legend tells of four *maile* sisters: brittle *maile*, luxuriant *maile*, greedy *maile*, and sweet-leafed *maile*. The Pana'ewa district of the Big Island was noted for the fragrant forests, with *maile*, *'ie'ie*, and *hala*. Fishermen far out at sea could smell the fragrance wafting off the land. There are several forms of *maile* in Hawai'i, with leaves of different sizes and shapes and various amounts of fragrance. *Maile* relatives in the genus *Alyxia* also grow naturally in parts of Polynesia and Southeast Asia.

Maile is a favorite and well-known native Hawaiian plant. It naturally inhabits Hawaiian mesic (medium amounts of rain) forests and true rain forests. Hula dancers know it as one of the plants sacred to Laka, goddess of the hula. Some say Laka could take the form of *maile*. *Maile*, along with *'ie'ie*, *hala pepe*, *palapalai*, and *'ōhi'a lehua*, is placed on the hula altar.

In the old days, *maile lau nui* (large-leafed *maile*) usually came from the Big Island, and *maile lau li'i* (small-leafed *maile*) from Kaua'i. Today, much of the *maile lau nui* sold in lei shops comes from Rarotonga and the other Cook islands. Someone who visited there told me that it lives on raised coral benches near the ocean.

Maile is in the same plant family as plumeria, and *maile* flowers look like miniature plumeria blossoms. Plumeria is native to Mexico and has a poisonous milky sap that you never want to get in your eyes; it even irritates the hands of some people. This sap protects plumeria from being eaten or bothered by the numerous animals native to Mexico. *Maile* also has a milky sap, but all it seems to do is enhance the fragrance. Thus, unfortunately, *maile* is readily chomped and trampled by introduced animals.

PROPAGATION AND CARE: *Maile* seeds sprout readily. As the plant grows larger, it requires cool, moist upland conditions. It grows well in places like the upper Nu'uanu Valley and Wahiawā. It prefers shade and rich organic soil. One volunteer at Wahiawā Botanical Garden has it growing under her lychee tree. She has made dozens of leis from her own cultivated plants. This is first-rate conservation of native Hawaiian materials.

Maile *seeds are black and shiny when ripe and become green as they ripen. To grow* maile *from seeds, remove the thin fruit layer, soak the seeds overnight, and plant in a pot of clean potting mix. Water at least daily.*

Maile *flowers look like miniature plumerias, to which they are related. The milky, poisonous sap of plumeria from Mexico protects it from grazing animals. The milky sap of Hawaiian* maile *only enhances the perfume of this choice lei and hula plant.*

Cherished vines of fragrant maile *are embraced by lei makers, hula dancers, and Hawaiian plant lovers. More gardening and horticultural research is needed to make* maile *easy to grow and plentiful in Hawai'i gardens.*

LANDSCAPE USE: *Maile* can grow as a vine or as a shrub that tends to vine (scientists call it a "woody liana"). Give it some attractive support to twine around; nicely shaped branches, a small tree, or an attractive trellis work well. It likes semishady growing conditions, in a cool, moist, upper-elevation garden.

PESTS: Once in a while, scale insects attach themselves to the stems and new leaves and suck sap. Don't overfertilize, treat the scale with garden insecticides or insecticidal soap, or scrape them off with a fingernail or old toothbrush.

OTHER USES: *Maile* makes a favorite, precious lei. To gather *maile* for a lei, choose fresh stems in a flush of growth. Twist or bite the stem at the edge of the soft tip growth and the tougher lower growth. Then strip off the bark. Knot the vine pieces together in a method called *nipu'u* or *hipu'u.*

Collecting *maile* is an enjoyable and fragrant experience, but it is devastating to the forest. After *maile* pickers have been through, a year of new growth is removed and bare stems remain, topping the old growth. Good pickers pick one here and one farther on, but there are so many people in modern Hawai'i that we can't all pick *maile* from the wild. Graduations, inaugurations, and other special events seriously strip the forest. The answer is for lei makers to grow their own *maile* and carefully harvest that.

*F*ERNS

Ferns are many gardeners' favorite, especially here in Hawai'i. They grow lushly and beautifully. The new fronds unfurl so gracefully and seemingly miraculously. They are favorites from time immemorial of hula dancers and lei makers. We have many nice introduced species and even more native Hawaiian species that surely deserve a special place in your heart and in your garden.

I have mentioned just a few of the more commonly grown and available ferns here. For more information on ferns, see the great book by my friend Kathy Valier called *Ferns of Hawai'i*. She has graciously allowed me to share some of her information and research, especially on the meanings of Hawaiian fern terminology.

PALAPALAI, PALAI

SCIENTIFIC NAME: *Microlepia strigosa*
FAMILY: Dennstaedtiaceae

Endemic

Palapalai is a favorite of lei makers and hula dancers. Leis are made from *palapalai* alone or in combination with other native Hawaiian and introduced plant materials. *Palapalai* is one of the plants sacred to Laka, goddess of hula and of the forest. It grows well in semishady, wet sites. It likes a rich organic soil with good drainage, so you can add compost and cinders if your soil is lacking. It is fairly easy to grow, and lots of Hawai'i gardeners grow it successfully. It is usually available at garden centers, and horticulturists are growing it from tissue culture.

Palapalai is also called *palai* and *palai'ula* (the latter refers to the dark black stalk of the fern). In the Hawaiian language, *palai* means to turn one's face away in bashfulness.

You can usually find this fern in moist forests, except where it has been overpicked by careless lei makers or trampled and rooted by feral pigs.

PROPAGATION AND CARE: The easiest way to grow *palapalai* is to buy a plant. *Palapalai* will grow in a pot, but it will be happier in the ground. If you have a pot of *palapalai* that seems densely packed with fronds and roots, use a slender, sharp saw to slice straight through the root ball, dividing it in halves or thirds. Replant the pieces in their own pots or in the ground to start your *palapalai* patch.

LANDSCAPE USE: *Palapalai* is a beautiful complement for most Hawaiian gardens. Many *akamai* gardeners plant it in a shady spot

These palapalai *fronds in a Wahiawā garden are being nurtured for that special lei-giving occasion.*

A hapa-haole *planting at Wahiawā Botanical Garden. Mondo "grass" (Japanese lily turf) forms a protective lei around the lei-makers' favorite: palapalai* fern.

Palapalai lau nui *grows in a moist, native tree–filled gulch in the Wai'anae Mountains in the Honouliuli preserve. "Dry forests" of Hawai'i are not dry if filled with natural layers of native plants, hugging and insulating every growing niche and capturing and filtering the rainwater that does fall.*

Adorned with pala'a, *or lace fern. Photo by Jean Cote.*

near the house and close to the hose, so they are reminded to give it a drink. Lei makers like mass plantings so their lei-making material is close at hand and so they can admire these lovely ferns gracefully swaying in the passing breezes. It makes a nice ground cover and is a good accent or specimen plant.

PESTS: Caterpillars sometimes attack *palapalai*, and this happens rather rapidly. You will notice part of the frond is missing. You can look for the culprit and pick it off and smash it. You can also spray with Sevin or other insecticides labeled for ferns.

OTHER USES: *Palapalai* has a great fragrance. When you wear it in a lei or in your hair, you and those around you can enjoy the fragrance. As the lei dries, the fragrance continues. It is significant in the hula, being sacred to the goddess Laka, and is one of the important plants that adorn the hula altar.

PALA'Ā, LACE FERN

SCIENTIFIC NAME: *Sphenomeris chinensis* or *Odontosoria chinensis*
FAMILY: Lindsaeaceae

Indigenous to Hawai'i, other parts of Polynesia, and east Asia

Pala'ā grows in the mountains and forests of Hawai'i and also at lower, moist elevations. You find it growing in rich brown forest soil, and it also loves red dirt. Often it will be one of the few Hawaiian plants that comes up on a red dirt road-cut embankment. These red dirt soils have few plant nutrients except for lots of iron and aluminum oxides (the iron is what makes the dirt red). Not many plants like this kind of soil, but *pala'ā* and other native ferns like *uluhe* thrive in it.

    Known as *pala'ā* or *palapala'ā* to the Hawaiians, the lace fern is indigenous to Hawai'i, other parts of Polynesia, and east Asia. It has a rhizome, or underground rooted stem, from which the fronds arise. The fronds can grow to up to 2 feet long under good conditions. If given enough moisture, *pala'ā* can thrive in full sun. It also does well in well-watered shade. The fronds are a lighter yellow-green and the stems a more reddish color when grown in the sun. The fronds are subdivided three times, and the smallest divisions are wedge shaped.

PROPAGATION AND CARE: This is not a plant you will find in most nurseries—yet. But with all the tissue culture success by awesome plantsman Greg Koob and his fellow horticulturists at Lyon Arboretum, we are seeing it offered for sale now. They grow it in tissue culture from the spores found on the undersides of the leaves. Once you have a plant in a pot, water it well and fertilize it moderately. It will thrive in the ground if you have rich brown soil or, preferably, red dirt soil. If you live in an area with sandy soil, you probably should not plant it in the ground. Liquid fertilizer such as fish emulsion is good for *pala'ā*.

LANDSCAPE USE: *Pala'ā* is quite pretty in the landscape. You can plant it as a ground cover, and it is great under *'ōhi'a lehua* or *hāpu'u*. You can plant a specimen or a whole patch for your garden's beauty and for that special lei-making occasion.

PESTS: *Pala'ā* has few pests.

OTHER USES: The Hawaiians made reddish brown or dark brown dye from the old, lacy fronds. *Pala'ā* is said to have been worn around the hips of Hi'iaka, the favorite younger sister of Pele. Hi'iaka used *pala'ā* to trip and entangle the *mo'o*, or dragons, which in times of old tried to hinder her long trip to reunite Lohi'au of Kaua'i with Pele. *Pala'ā* was used to treat female ailments; the fern dispensed with the problem the way it had dispensed with the *mo'o*.

Pala'ā is made into a lei using the *hili*, or *hilo*, technique, which is a braiding or plaiting method with only one type of plant material. It is also made into *haku* when used with other plants, and *wili*, the winding method, using a backing.

Looking at this pala'ā *frond, you can see why* pala'ā *is called the "lace fern."*

KUPUKUPU, 'ŌKUPUKUPU, NI'ANI'AU

SCIENTIFIC NAME: *Nephrolepis cordifolia*
FAMILY: Nephrolepidaceae

Indigenous to Hawai'i, other areas of the tropics, and as far north and south as Japan and New Zealand

Kupukupu, also known as *'ōkupukupu* and on Ni'ihau as *ni'ani'au*, is an attractive and tough native Hawaiian sword fern. It has dark green fronds 6 inches to over 2 feet tall, depending on the plant's age and growing conditions. It grows so thickly and profusely, even aggressively in some places (like my Wahiawā garden), that you almost wonder if it is really a native Hawaiian. This very aggressiveness is, however, what makes it so wonderful in the landscape. Wouldn't you rather have a tough, beautiful, thick, and verdantly green fern that you can cut for leis, flower arrangements, or a graveside visit than a nasty old high-maintenance fertilizer-, water-, and pesticide-devouring lawn?

Kupukupu has another great attribute, rare in Hawaiian ferns—it is a drought-tolerant, or less thirsty, plant. Thus it is great for your xeriscape garden. It spreads by its running roots and also has little bulblets on the roots that store water for the plant in times of scarcity; these also serve as a propagule for new fern plants.

PROPAGATION AND CARE: Lyon Arboretum is tissue culturing and offering *kupukupu* for sale. Once you get a plant, it grows and spreads vigorously. You can pull out new plants and place them in other parts of your garden or share them with friends. We should be seeing this fern in the nursery trade soon.

Kupukupu makes a nice groundcover planting for ma'o hau hele *at Lyon Arboretum on O'ahu.*

LANDSCAPE USE: *Kupukupu* can grow on the ground, amid rocks and boulders, and even up the trunks of trees in moist areas. It loves to send its rhizomes in and around *hāpuʻu* or even tough Australian tree fern trunks. This fern also forms a wonderful, thick ground cover. You can see it growing profusely and attractively under native hibiscus at Lyon Arboretum.

We have been testing *kupukupu* in dryland gardens. One garden in Makiki has black sand for soil, and the *kupukupu* is planted in a place where the hose rarely reaches. Still, it is gorgeous and makes a nice open groundcover patch of fern. Recently we planted some in a sandy-soiled Waikīkī garden (at the Hale Koa Hotel), and it too is growing well and looking luxuriant. We did amend the soil with lots of rich organic matter, and we have an automatic irrigation system and a devoted gardener who watered the new ferns every morning to get them established in their new coastal garden home.

Kupukupu also thrives in pots. You can grow it on your lanai or in the garden of your rented home. You can always dig up some of the plant when you have to move—and leave some for your gracious landlord, or the next resident.

PESTS: *Kupukupu* has few pests.

OTHER USES: This fern is great in leis, long-lasting and good-looking in flower arrangements, and nice added to flowers worn in your hair. It is placed on the hula altar to encourage the sprouting (*kupu*) of knowledge by the dancers.

KUPUKUPU, PAMOHO

SCIENTIFIC NAME: *Nephrolepis exaltata*
FAMILY: Nephrolepidaceae

Indigenous to Hawaiʻi, other areas of the tropics, and as far north and south as Japan and New Zealand

This is another Hawaiian fern known as *kupukupu*, and some people call it *pamoho*. The fronds are larger, lighter green, and shinier than *Nephrolepis cordifolia*, and smooth and glossy in comparison to introduced "Boston" ferns, which are also members of the genus *nephrolepis*. This fern is quite handsome—in the landscape, in leis, and in flower arrangements. Under the right conditions, the fronds can grow up to 4 feet long.

PROPAGATION AND CARE: This fern is easy to grow from a small plant. You can dig up one from a friend's patch or buy it at a plant sale sponsored by one of the local botanical gardens. Horticulturists are tissue-culturing it, so it should be available through your favorite nursery before too long. Like any good consumer, you should ask your local garden center to carry this and other native Hawaiian plants. Take a wish list with you when you go plant shopping.

LANDSCAPE USE: *Kupukupu* is an attractive fern in a groundcover planting, as a specimen, or in a large, decorative pot. It grows in the shade or in semishade.

Kupukupu *has large, glossy light-green leaves, favored for leis.*

PESTS: *Kupukupu* has few pests.

OTHER USES: *Kupu* means "to sprout" in Hawaiian. This fern was symbolic of sprouting knowledge and was used to decorate and give meaning to hula altars. A hula chant refers to the fragrant *kupukupu* that grows on Kānehoa (named for the father of Pele), in the Wai'anae mountain range on O'ahu. When dancers adorn their wrists and ankles with *lei kupukupu*, they chant, "the fragrant *kupukupu* of the heights of Kānehoa."

HĀPU'U, HĀPU'U PULU, HAWAIIAN TREE FERN

SCIENTIFIC NAME: *Cibotium glaucum*, C. spp.
FAMILY: Dicksoniaceae

Endemic

Hāpu'u is known to Hawaiians as the "mother of the forest." This is partially because many other plants, like *'ōhi'a lehua*, *ōlapa*, mosses, and often ferns, get their start in life on the moist, fibrous trunks of *hāpu'u*. Young *hāpu'u* that don't have a trunk are called *hāpu'upu'u*.

Hāpu'u have bright green fronds that are whitish on the underside. The common species has golden *pulu* (hairs) covering the trunk and encasing the young fronds as they develop and uncurl.

Botanists recognize four species of Hawaiian *hāpu'u*. One that is easy to pick out in the forest is *hāpu'u 'i'i*, or *Cibotium menziesii*. Some old-time hikers call this the "boy *hāpu'u*." It has stiff black hairs covering the bases of the fronds and upper trunk.

In the past, *hāpu'u* was one of the most common plants in our Hawaiian rain forests. *'Ōhi'a lehua* growing in association with *hāpu'u* is one of the Islands' main forest types. These foundation plants serve as shade, shelter, and moisture sinks for other shade-loving trees, plants, and ferns, and they also provide food and shelter for native birds and land snails.

These hāpu'u *sporelings are growing at Mt. Ka'ala on O'ahu. New plants grow from spores.*

PROPAGATION AND CARE: *Hāpu'u* can be grown from side shoots on the main trunk and by spores (a fern's form of "seeds"). You can grow your own *hāpu'u* plant, or even a fern forest, if you provide the plants with the right environment. They like a rich, organic, well-drained soil and lots of water. You can buy the young plants or uproot trunks from a nursery.

LANDSCAPE USE: *Hāpu'u* does fine in full sun or partial shade with abundant moisture; it does not thrive in deep shade. It can tolerate some salt spray, but the fronds don't stand up well in windy areas.

Buy *hāpu'u* from a reputable nursery. Do not dig them out of the

Hāpuʻu iʻi is called the "boy" hāpuʻu *by some* kolohe *aunties. The dark, stiff hairs on the fronds of this* hāpuʻu *do have a male look to them. It is actually a different species. There are five native Hawaiian species of* hāpuʻu, *or* Cibotium.

forest. They rarely survive being yanked out of their native home, and you don't want to accelerate the environmental damage.

Hāpuʻu can reach heights of 15 to 20 feet, but this doesn't happen in most gardens. Its arching fronds can reach lengths of 9 feet. They are green above and light green or tan below, depending on the species.

PESTS: *Hāpuʻu* has few pests.

OTHER USES: The early Hawaiians, excellent botanists that they were, recognized the different species, just as botanists do today. They called them *hāpuʻu*, *hāpuʻu ʻiʻi* and *hāpuʻu pulu*. *Pulu* is the silky red-brown "wool" that covers the trunk and leaf bases. The Hawaiians used *pulu* for stuffing pillows and mattresses, as wound dressing, and for embalming the dead. *Pulu* was one of Hawaiʻi's first exports; it was sent to bed down the miners during the Gold Rush. The starch found inside the trunk was famine food in old Hawaiʻi, and it was also used to feed pigs. Today this is what feral pigs are after when they knock down and chomp entire *hāpuʻu* forests. Early Hawaiians also cooked and ate the young fronds, or fiddleheads.

The fronds make an excellent soil mulch and were once used to enrich the soil for *kalo*, *ʻuala*, and other crops. You can use old fronds the same way. Cut them off and lay them around the base of the *hāpuʻu* or other plants. Don't put them in the trash (and overstuff our landfills with useful material).

Because of land development and clearing, destructive feral pigs and goats, and the demand for *hāpuʻu* products by the horticulture industry, our unique Hawaiian tree ferns are becoming less common. This is a shame, for they grow fairly slowly; under ideal rain forest conditions it takes about ten years to grow one foot of *hāpuʻu* trunk! Many orchid and bromeliad growers use slabs, chunks, or shreds of *hāpuʻu* to grow their plants on. This is not really a good use of *hāpuʻu*; rocks, coconut fiber, and other porous materials work just as well without destroying our forests. Too much harvesting of *hāpuʻu* wrecks the balance of the forest and could even affect our water supplies. Healthy native Hawaiian forests catch rain and even vagrant wisps of fog and mist, use and filter that moisture, and then let it trickle down through the rocks to our underground water supplies.

CAUTION: We shouldn't use another common landscape tree fern, the Australian tree fern, anymore. The faster-growing, more drought-tolerant, hard-trunked Australian is endangering our Hawaiian forests. The spores from the ones in our garden are carried by the wind up to the forests, where the spores sprout and grow many vigorous invading tree fern plants. According to Maui naturalist Paul Higashino, in areas like upper Kīpahulu, where the rain forest is mainly pristine and intact, dense Australian fern stands are taking over, drying out the area and preventing native regrowth. It seems harsh, but chop down that Aussie and replant with native Hawaiian *hāpuʻu*. Don't mulch the alien fronds; put them in a trash bag or they could cause more invasions.

Growing Native Hawaiian Plants

'ĒKAHA, BIRD'S-NEST FERN

SCIENTIFIC NAME: *Asplenium nidus*
FAMILY: Polypodiaceae

Indigenous to Hawai'i and other parts of Polynesia westward to Africa

'Ēkaha, the bird's-nest fern, is one native Hawaiian plant that can be found in many garden shops and nurseries. It is a fantastic and versatile landscape plant and also makes a good plant for homes and other interior spaces. It is somewhat drought tolerant, and this adds to its versatility.

In the wild, 'ēkaha is found growing on the ground or perched way up on big boulders or in trees. You can see it growing on the ground and in trees at the Wahiawa Botanical Garden.

'Ēkaha is indigenous to Hawai'i, but not endemic: it got to Hawai'i without the help of people, but it also grows as a native in other parts of the world from Polynesia westward to Africa.

Huge 'ēkaha *line the mossy cliffs of this wet, remote, and protected crater at Kalaupapa on Moloka'i.*

There is a gulch in Honouliuli Preserve in the Wai'anae mountains called 'Ēkahanui. I went in with botanist Joel Lau and horticulturist Clark Leavitt a few years ago, expecting to find huge overtopping cathedrals of 'ēkaha growing in the trees. Sadly, there were only a few, growing here and there in the tallest, skinniest unclimbable trees. The famous 'ēkaha of old had either succumbed to drought or, worse yet, been carried off by impatient, greedy people. Hawaiian plants should not be dug out of the forest or ripped off trees. Buy a small plant from a nursery (where they are grown from spores) and patiently nurture and grow it.

The fronds of 'ēkaha are long, smooth, somewhat leathery, and narrow-oblong in shape. They grow to 2 to 4 feet long or longer and are 3 to 8 inches wide. They have a prominent, dark brown or black raised midrib in their center. The mature fronds have dark patterns of raised lines on the underside, which give an attractive and interesting appearance to the plants, especially when viewed from below. These lines are leaf veins that cover and protect the sori, which contain spores. Ferns are ancient plants, and they do not have seeds. New plants grow from spores in a complicated life cycle requiring lots of moisture.

'Ēkaha is in the Polypodiaceae fern family, along with such other native Hawaiian ferns as *hō'i'o kula, kikawaiō, 'iwa'iwa, pai'ā, kīlau, pala'ā, kupukupu,* and *'ama'u.*

PROPAGATION AND CARE: The easiest way to grow 'ēkaha is to buy a plant from a nursery or garden center. Keep it regularly watered and transplant it, into successively larger pots, when it gets too big for the current pot.

You can put your 'ēkaha up in a tree and grow it as it is found in the Hawaiian forest. Select a large crotch or horizontal branch that will support and display the 'ēkaha. Take it out of the pot and spread

'Ēkaha grow in profusion on the mossy pali of a wet lowland Moloka'i valley. The upward view is spectacular.

the roots out in a fan shape. Tie the *'ēkaha* firmly into the tree with old pantyhose or garden stretch tape. Water it well to get it established, and then water at least twice a week.

The more difficult way to grow *'ēkaha* is from spores. Collect a leaf with mature spores. Put it upside down on clean paper or in a paper bag. Collect the spores in a day or two and place them on moist sterile medium in a clean pot. Mist daily and keep in a shady, protected spot. Transplant the sporelings to their own pot when they have several sets of fronds.

Horticulturists are also using tissue culture or micropropagation to grow *'ēkaha* and other native Hawaiian ferns from spores.

'Ēkaha responds well to foliar fertilizer and does especially well when fertilized with liquid fish emulsion. Pour this over the fronds and into the medium about twice a month. It also likes slow-release and organic fertilizers, which should be incorporated into the potting medium when you repot. You can also topdress with slow-release or organic fertilizer mixed with well-rotted compost.

LANDSCAPE USE: *'Ēkaha* is attractive as a ground cover or accent plant in a partially shady landscape. You can plant it in the ground, or you can keep it in a pot and hide the pot with the surrounding plants or by mounding media or decorative rocks around the pot.

It is particularly striking perched up in a tree. This gives an exotic look to the landscape and is not very hard to accomplish.

PESTS: *'Ēkaha* has few pests.

OTHER USES: The midrib of *'ēkaha* was traditionally used for several decorative and craft purposes. The ancient Hawaiians decorated *lau hala* items like hats, baskets, and small mats with the midribs. In the carefully planned canoe-building ceremony, the selected tree was ceremonially cut, and then the stump was covered with *'ēkaha* before the trunk was shaped with an adze into a canoe.

'IWA'IWA, MAIDENHAIR FERN

SCIENTIFIC NAME: *Adiantum capillus-veneris*
FAMILY: Adiantaceae

Indigenous to Hawai'i and warm temperate regions as far north as South Carolina and as far south as Australia (but not to New Zealand)

When you go hiking, you find lots of maidenhair fern gracefully covering wet banks with its fine, misty fronds. These plants are all so fragile and beautiful, they surely must be native. I always thought so. Fern expert Tim Flynn of the National Tropical Botanical Garden set me straight. There is one type of native maidenhair fern—*'iwa'iwa*—but it is not commonly seen. Most types around Hawai'i today were brought here by people and have spread by wind- and water-carried spores. Now they grow successfully in many wild places and look native—like many other plants that have made a good home for themselves

Native Hawaiian maidenhair fern. Note the shape of the spore cases: oblong or rectangular, with deeply cut frond sections. Photo by Robert Hobdy.

in Hawaiʻi thanks to us, our penchant for carrying plants with us on our travels, and the many varied and hospitable microclimates of these precious islands.

ʻIwaʻiwa grows out on the ends of Kauaʻi's dry ridges, like Kaʻawiki and Polihale. The plants grow on north-facing ridges and thrive in the wet times of year, then die back in the baking summer heat. They also grow hanging down in the dry and wet caves on the north shore of Kauaʻi. ʻIwaʻiwa likes the moist faces of rocks and enjoys shade, but it also grows in harsh places that are too rugged for introduced competitors. You see it along the coast sometimes at Hanakāpīʻai. It can grow right in the salt spray. ʻIwaʻiwa tends to be smaller and less branched than the introduced maidenhair ferns. Its leaf lobes are deeply cut, and the spore cases are rectangular. This Hawaiian native also grows naturally in many other tropical places. It is getting crowded out by the more aggressive introduced maidenhairs. Since it has a tough nature in the wild, more of us should try to grow the native Hawaiian ʻiwaʻiwa.

ʻIwa is the Hawaiian name for the great frigatebird. ʻIwaʻiwa refers to the graceful way maidenhair sways and dips and dives in the smallest of breezes. This graceful swaying inspired a chant and hula.

PROPAGATION AND CARE: Maidenhair ferns are easy to grow. You can buy a plant from a nursery and later repot it into large pots or into the ground. You can divide maidenhairs to make more plants. They are one fern that you can safely cut back, to clean up the patch or reinvigorate the pot, and let the new growth resprout, but be sure to water the ferns well after you do this. It is better to selectively cut off the few old junky-looking fronds, but if you have a big patch in the landscape you can cut back more aggressively.

Maidenhair also don't mind being grown indoors. The moist, humid air in a bathroom is a favorite place to grow them. They like to be fertilized, especially with dilute liquid fertilizer such as Miracle-Gro, time-released fertilizers, and my favorite for ferns, fish emulsion.

LANDSCAPE USE: Maidenhair ferns are attractive in the landscape. Their small, delicate scale makes them particularly suitable for the home garden. Planted beds of ʻiwaʻiwa are gorgeous; it can be used for accent, and it makes a fairly tough ground cover. You can also keep it in attractive pots displayed around the garden.

PESTS: ʻIwaʻiwa has few pests.

OTHER USES: Like the black-stemmed midribs of ʻēkaha (the bird's-nest fern), the attractive black, wiry stems of ʻiwaʻiwa are used in ornamental craftwork such as plaited lau hala baskets and purses.

HOW TO TELL THE HAWAIIAN MAIDENHAIR FERN FROM THE ALIEN ONES THAT ALSO ARE FOUND GROWING ALONG OUR HIKING TRAILS AND IN THE FORESTS:

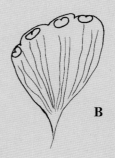

The native Hawaiian variety (figures A and C) has spore cases that are oblong or rectangular and deeply cut frond sections.

The alien ferns (figure B) have spore cases that are oval or heart shaped with less deeply cut frond sections.

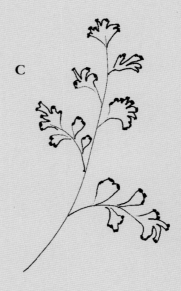

ULUHE, UNUHE, "LAND-HEALING" FERN, FALSE STAGHORN FERN

SCIENTIFIC NAME: *Dicranopteris linearis*
FAMILY: Gleicheniaceae

Uluhe fern covers the pristine mountains of Hawai'i with the most enchanting, refreshing light green color. From far away one might think that a perfect lawn was creating such a lush green. Up close *uluhe* is a rambling fern that can disguise sheer drop-offs, steep *pali*, or pits in the land. This is one of the many reasons that it is wise to stay on the trail when hiking in Hawai'i.

Uluhe is an indigenous fern; there is also an endemic subspecies, *Dicranopteris linearis f. emarginata*, which is usually found higher up the mountain than the typical form. The endemic form is more fuzzy looking, with light brown-golden hairs, or as fern expert Dr. Daniel Palmer says in his excellent fern manual *Hawai'i Ferns and Fern Allies*: "heavy wooly hairiness of its fronds and slightly emarginate segment tips" densely covered with wooly down.

LANDSCAPE USE: This fern is rarely cultivated or planted in the landscape. However, *akamai* gardeners who are gifted with land that has *uluhe* growing on it are wise to leave it alone. The color is unique and breathtaking. A patch of *uluhe* on a steep slope or unbulldozed rain forest land is the easiest thing in the world to maintain; just leave it alone, admire it, and if fire is a threat in your area, cut off the dry brown fronds. If fire is not a problem, leave the brown fronds on for their interest and beauty.

Patricia Rouen, who is restoring the land she owns in Anahola, Kaua'i, to a Hawaiian rain forest, encourages her *uluhe* and plants other choice native plants like *hāpu'u*, *'ōhi'a lehua*, and *koki'o ke'oke'o* in and amidst the *uluhe*. The land-healing fern makes a good "nursery" for the other plants, complete with mulch and shade to shelter other plants and keep down the weeds.

PROPAGATION: Our fabulous growers of native plants and ferns are working on propagating this fern from spores. This would be a great living tool to use in landscape restoration and erosion control.

You can also dig up a big clump of *uluhe* roots, organic soil and all, and replant it in the garden. This is not recommended unless the area you're taking it from will be bulldozed or the *uluhe* otherwise wiped out. I tried this during construction at Ho'omaluhia Botanical Garden. The area was due to be scraped and graded for a new road, so I came in ahead of the bulldozer and dug out some *uluhe* with a balling spade. I immediately transferred it to a nursery flat and took it back to the shady fern section of the greenhouse. I watered it well right away, and then daily. It grew for several years in the nursery, but we did not have a good enough irrigation system to try planting it back in the field.

PESTS: *Uluhe* is a fairly pest-free fern. It grows so well that many think it is an introduced fern (especially those hikers in shorts whose

Uluhe, *the land-healing fern, grows with* 'ōhia lehua *and* koa *on a windswept rainforest ridge. Photo by Liz Huppman.*

bare legs get poked and scratched by dry, broken-off *uluhe* fronds). Some people are skeptical about whether it is a native Hawaiian plant at all, because of its rambunctious, almost weedy growth. The late, great botanist Dr. Raymond Fosberg once told me that "only in Hawai'i does it seem to want to take over the land, scrambling over everything in its path. In other areas where it is native, it is a much more demure, self-contained fern."

In about 1993, the two-spotted leafhopper, a pest that had been here awhile and was expanding its population, reached epidemic proportions, and many plants suffered from it. This pest has toxic saliva and in high numbers can kill plants. *Uluhe* was particularly hard hit, with whole patches turning black and dying. Weeds could now sprout in areas once thick and lush with *uluhe*.

Thanks largely to the groundbreaking work of entomologist and Integrated Pest Management (IPM) expert Lynne Constantinides, during an urban forestry project at Ho'omaluhia we discovered many new insect pests on native Hawaiian plants. She suggests controlling the two-spotted leafhopper by using a systemic insecticide and monitoring for damage. Keep the soil and the plants healthy and you will have less damage.

'AMA'U, AMA'UMA'U

SCIENTIFIC NAME: *Sadleria*
FAMILY: Gleicheniaceae

Endemic

This rain forest fern is a tree fern like *hāpu'u*, but the fronds are only singly pinnate. New fronds come out a gorgeous pink or bronze, like the *liko* (new leaf clusters) of *'ōhi'a lehua*, *lama*, and other native Hawaiian plants.

'Ama'u isn't cultivated as widely as *hāpu'u*, yet it is handsome in gardens. It does best in cool, *mauka* upland gardens and native forests. One place you do see it in landscapes and gardens is in Volcano on the Big Island. There it thrives and is seen fairly often in *hapa*-Japanese gardens along with *hāpu'u* and *'ōhi'a lehua*, as well as camellias, azaleas, Japanese maples, and *kwai fah*.

'Ama'u has a smaller, narrower trunk than *hāpu'u* and is a shorter, smaller tree fern overall. *Hāpu'u* and *'ama'u* are gorgeous mixed together, giving a real Hawaiian rain forest feel and look to a garden.

PROPAGATION: *'Ama'u* can be grown from spores. Specialty growers should be encouraged to do this. *'Ama'u* grown from spores would be a real asset for our gardens and for restoring and perpetuating Hawaiian forest ecosystems for the future.

'Ama'u should never be dug up from the wild, unless the land is to be bulldozed. A better option is to carefully dig it up and then carefully replant after the 'dozer is done.

PESTS: The biggest threat to *'ama'u* is people, who bulldoze the

The newly emerging and unfolding fronds of 'ama'u *fern are a bright coral pink or red. These colors are protective for the vulnerable new fern fronds.*

forests where it grows; develop, burn, introduce cattle and feral pigs, etc. In the garden, watch for pests that sometimes attack other ferns, such as mealybugs, caterpillars, and leafhoppers. If you keep the plants and their root-filled trunks moist and the soil "well fed" with organics, 'ama'u should be happy.

'IHI'IHI LAUAKEA

SCIENTIFIC NAME: *Marsilea villosa*
FAMILY: Marsiliaceae

Endemic

Before people started dredging and filling our vital, life-giving wetlands, Hawai'i's environment was a lot wetter, with natural wetlands, *kalo* patches, and Hawaiian fishponds. *'Ihi'ihi lauakea*, a unique 4-fronded water fern, was found fairly commonly then, on the banks of *lo'i kalo* (taro patches), and in wet, wild lowlands. Today it is found in only a few sites in the wild. Fortunately, many gardeners grow it and share it with other growers, perpetuating this rare and unusual native plant. It looks like a four-leaf clover, but you can tell that it is a fern by looking at the newest frond. It furls like the scroll of a violin and is called a fiddlehead. 'Most all ferns have new fronds that open, uncurl, and grow in this circular fashion.

It is named *'ihi'ihi lauakea* after the low volcanic crater on the flanks of Koko Head, above Hanauma Bay, where some of the fern still grows.

My friend Marie Brugmann, one of the best botanists in Hawai'i, wrote her masters thesis on this fern and continues to monitor and study it. In 1987, when we got a good soaking *kona* storm—the first in about fourteen years—the pool in which the fern grows flooded and we came out joyfully to celebrate the burgeoning life therein. The fern was up and unfurled, with fronds floating on the water, which was thigh deep in places. Under these conditions the ferns "have sex." In normal dry conditions they hang onto life somewhat precariously, and only grow vegetatively. They need standing water for the fern spores to release from the hard, dried-up sporocarps. The spores unite and mix in the water and plantlets form from this union.

Also in the vernal pool were clam shrimp and other arthropods that also come to life only when there is a good flood.

For years we tended and weeded the patch, in a cooperative volunteer partnership of The Nature Conservancy of Hawai'i, UH-Mānoa, and the city parks department, with excellent results. We planted other natives like *wiliwili* and *'ilima* around the edges, with mixed results (the location is very windy, with dry and salty air and soil). We kept the ferns weeded of alien grasses, morning glories, and other invasive plants. The fern patch thrived under this vigilant horticultural care and maintenance. The ferns could just not compete with the weeds on their own.

LANDSCAPE USE: *'Ihi* is a fabulous addition to a water garden.

'Ihi'ihi lauakea *grows in a planting with round protective rocks at Hanauma Bay Education Center. The rocks and an enfolding planting of* naupaka kahakai *protect this rare and choice fern from the hordes who visit the Hanauma Bay Marine Preserve, a snorkeling wonderland.*

Sexual fronds of 'ihi'ihi lauakea *float on the water after the great soaking Kona storm of 1985.*

You can grow the plants in well-watered ornamental jugs and pots. You can grow them in Tupperware! You can grow them along the banks of your *lo'i kalo* as they were often found growing in old Hawai'i.

Imaginative gardeners and landscape architects and designers will find many uses for this unique water fern. The 4 fronds should be lucky for their clients! Many people will insist that it is a 4-leaf clover, even after you show them the emerging fern frond.

PROPAGATION: *'Ihi'ihi lauakea* can be grown by divisions, from plants growing in the garden. Lots of people grow it now, and good gardeners propagate and share with others. Keep records of those you gave or sold plants to so you can re-collect them if yours die.

This fern can also be grown from spores. It is an interesting and exciting process to see new life emerge from old dried-up sporocarps.

PESTS: Weeds, especially alien grasses, are a pest of this fern and need to be kept under control. Watch your plants for other garden pests and control them. Monitor your watering closely to make sure the fern does not dry out and perish.

Horticulture and wetland restoration are good luck for this rare fern, which looks like a four-leaf clover. Note the new fiddlehead, unfolding in typical fern fashion on this 'ihi'ihi lauakea.

MOA

SCIENTIFIC NAME: *Psilotum nudum*
FAMILY: Psilotaceae (whisk fern family)

Indigenous

Moa is a primitive, fernlike plant. To the Hawaiians the wiry stems looked like chicken feet—thus the name *moa* (chicken).

Hawaiian *keiki* played a game with this plant. They would hold a *moa* stem and interlock it with the other player's stem. Then they'd pull them apart. Whoever had a more intact stem won and would then have to crow like a rooster.

The *moa* stems can grow to about a foot high and as wide or wider. They are green and wiry. The spores are yellow, and sometimes the stems turn from green into a very attractive yellow-orange.

Primitive plants like this don't make seeds to grow new plants from. They spread by spores. The spores of *moa* are yellow. These *moa* spores were used like talcum powder in old Hawai'i—to prevent chafing under the *malo*. The stem, which had cathartic properties, was brewed into a tea.

Moa is an indigenous Hawaiian plant. It is also found growing naturally elsewhere all over the tropics. It grows in dry and moist environments and will grow on the ground, amidst rocks, on trees, and in stone walls. The roots of *moa* have a cooperative, symbiotic fungus that helps them grow. (Orchids grow this way also, and so do many other forest trees and plants.)

PROPAGATION: Don't even try to grow *moa*; it comes up where

Moa is a prehistoric fern relative. It is prized for lei making and hair adornment.

Lei moa. *Photo by Jean Cote.*

Lei moa. *Photo by Jean Cote.*

it likes. It just grows wild. I have tried to grow *moa* and it's possible—sort of. It seems happier coming up where it wants to come up. Now isn't that scientific?

When I was working at the Kalihi yard of the Honolulu Board of Water Supply, there was lots of *moa* in a waste area that was scheduled for clearing. I dug the plants up and transplanted them to individual pots using different kinds of media. They lived but did not grow and flourish. This is a good problem for the new crop of young and innovative as well as the old-fashioned propagators to explore further. *Moa* is a simple plant and should be simple to grow. It happily comes up in stone and CMU (concrete masonry unit) walls at the edges. There is a tall—probably 20-foot—moss rock wall at Kamehameha Schools that has a lush and gorgeous growth of *moa*. This makes a very attractive, natural, green, and "softened" Hawaiian stone wall. *Moa* will sometimes sprout in a pot with another plant. Often the two plants look good together and you can leave both or you can separate them.

LANDSCAPE USE: *Moa* is fab in a large decorative or clay pot. You can move it around like furniture to where you need it, or set it in a permanent location. Members of the Garden Club of Honolulu often grow amazing specimens for their competitive flower shows, held at the Honolulu Academy of Arts. These great gardeners have found the secret for nurturing *moa*!

OTHER USES: *Moa* is great to wear with flowers in your hair. We also found out accidentally that it may be a cut-flower life-enhancer when added to floral arrangements. (I had noticed that *moa* made great "traveling hair ornaments," along with my favorite yellow plumeria. They seemed to last well together if I put them in water after a hard day of traveling or attending a conference. My gardening *tūtū*, May Moir, came up with this use for *moa* at about the same time. We were casually testing it out, before she passed away. Try adding attractive pieces of *moa* to your flower arrangement and see if it lasts longer. At the least, *moa* is a pretty addition to the arrangement.)

$\mathcal{T}$REES

Many types of trees are native to Hawai'i. Why not plant one or two today? If you live in a high rise, get together with the community association and see where you might add a few more native trees to the common areas. Or get together a community group and plant native trees along your street, in a park, or in a nearby forest.

Some Hawaiian trees are rare and grow only in certain conditions, such as the wettest rain forests. The dryland forest, where the greatest number of species grows, is also where most people farm and construct buildings and highways, and the trees have been adversely affected. Many are now rare, or are very hard to grow, or grow slowly. The trees described here are those that have been found to be tough, attractive, and proven for use in landscapes.

HALA

SCIENTIFIC NAME: *Pandanus tectorius*
FAMILY: Pandanaceae (screw pine family)

Indigenous to Hawai'i, other parts of Polynesia, Melanesia, Micronesia, New Caledonia to northern Australia, new Guinea west to the Philippines, Moluccas, and Java

Hala has been given many names that try to describe its unique appearance: screw pine, for the spiraling leaf arrangement; walking tree, after the aerial roots (*ulehala*), which make the tree look as if it is about to walk around the garden; and pineapple tree, for the large reddish-orange fruit of female trees. Male trees have a white flower called *hīnano*.

Hala leaves are tough and very durable. They and the aerial roots are spiny. The trees can grow to 30 feet tall and 40 feet wide. They are found in lowland forests around the Islands but are particularly abundant from sea level to 2,000 feet on our windward coasts. They have a striking and unique form, and they thrive in salty, windy coastal conditions.

Recently discovered fossil evidence shows that *hala* is native to Hawai'i, though this most valued plant was also carried here in the sailing canoes of the ancient Polynesians. As Jan TenBruggencate, a local journalist interested in the Hawaiian environment, was walking along the beach in Hanalei, Kaua'i, he saw a strange-looking rock with an impression and striations. Going in for a closer look, he glanced up at the pali and saw a *hala* tree with fruit. The impression in the ancient rock that had eroded off the pali and split in half had been made by the fruit of a *hala* tree. Geologists and *hala* experts came out to verify the age and authenticity. The lava predated the Hawaiians, showing that *hala* is native to Hawai'i.

These graceful hala *flow down a wet slope in Limahuli Valley on the north shore of Kaua'i.*

Hala 'ula, *or red* hala, *growing at the nēnē exhibit at the Honolulu Zoo. This is a rare variety, famous in Hawaiian chant and mele.* Photo by Mark Tanimoto.

PROPAGATION AND CARE: *Hala* is easy to grow from seeds. Half bury the seeds in a pot of potting mix and water daily. It can also be grown from fairly large cuttings, stuck directly in the ground or in large pots and watered daily.

LANDSCAPE USE: *Hala* is one of our most beautiful and striking native trees, especially for coastal areas. Its unique Hawaiian tropical look rivals that of the *niu* (coconut), and *hala* is certainly easier and cheaper to maintain in a commercial landscape. It is tough and drought tolerant and can drink salt water with its stilt roots. It also thrives in wet areas. This tree should be planted a lot more than it is. It can grow in a wide range of climates. One of my favorites graces the grounds of a church up in Wahiawā.

PESTS: Mealy bugs and scale insects sometimes hide in the leaf crevices and suck the sap. Control these with insecticidal soap, insecticidal oils, or standard insecticide.

Ancient groves of hala *grow in Limahuli Botanical Garden, one of the gardens of the National Tropical Botanical Garden. Hala trees make an attractive and protective backdrop for other native Hawaiian plants that are nurtured in this garden.*

OTHER USES: The leaves of the *hala* tree (*lau hala*) are plaited into durable and highly prized hats, mats, baskets, jewelry, and thatching material. The Hawaiian home of old had sleeping mats, pillows, and, sometimes in fancy homes, even a ceiling made from *lau hala.*

The fruit is made into an attractive and fragrant lei, often in combination with *maile* or *laua'e.* Much is said, sung, and chanted about the fragrance of *pu hala* (the fruit). Fishermen far out at sea could smell the perfume wafting off the famous *hala* groves. It is a Hawaiian tradition to present a *hala* lei at the beginning of a new phase in someone's life. It is a lot of hard work to make a *hala* lei, because the hard and fibrous fruit must be cut, shaped, and drilled. *Lau hala* was used as a lei backing, and the fine fibers from the aerial roots were sometimes used for stringing leis such as *'ilima.*

The fruit, which smells good but is fibrous and has only a small edible fruit portion, was used as a famine food. The dried fruit was used as a paint brush for decorating kapa. It still makes a good paint brush for crafts today.

The male flower was used as an aphrodisiac in old Hawai'i. One simply sprinkled *hīnano* pollen onto the object of his or her desire. (They were sometimes not very subtle about expressing love.) This fragrant flower was laid between sheets of kapa to perfume it. Male trees have fairly solid trunks that were quite useful. Female trees have a hard outer cortex surrounding a soft pith.

Charcoal from *hala* wood was used in the various mixtures used to dye and waterproof canoes. The beaten aerial root tips were used as brushes to apply the concoction.

When Robert Louis Stevenson came to visit the Islands, he would sit under the *hala* to write, relax, or meditate.

Master papale lauhala *weaver Aunty Gladys Grace (left) is adorned with* lauhala *from her shirt to her hanging purse, bracelets, and hat. Her student Lola Spencer, of Moloka'i, sits beside her. Gwen Kamisugi, a member of a* lauhala hui, *is behind Lola, wearing green. Two O'ahu* lauhala *weavers sit under the historic* bo *tree (Ficus religiosa) in Foster Botanical Garden.*

WILIWILI, HAWAIIAN CORAL TREE, TIGER'S CLAW

SCIENTIFIC NAME: *Erythrina sandwicensis*
FAMILY: FABACEAE (bean family)

Endemic

Wiliwili is a tree of the dry leeward lowlands of Hawai'i. It grows fairly rapidly and has a mature height of about 30 feet. The flowers, which look like large pea blossoms, come in a variety of colors: apricot, chartreuse, white, yellow, red, chartreuse with an orange lip, and so on. The Hawaiian *Erythrina* is unique in the world for this wide variety of flower colors. It has a soft, light wood and beanlike pods that twist open during the wet season to reveal orange or red beanlike seeds. (*Wili* means to twist, and repeating a word is a way of emphasizing it. Thus, *wiliwili* means really twisty.)

The seeds of native Hawaiian wiliwili *are bright red or orange. Each pod usually has from one to three seeds.* Wiliwili *means "to twist and twist again." The pod twists and twists again to reveal and show off the seeds and then cast them loose to grow some distance away from the mother tree.*

PROPAGATION AND CARE: *Wiliwili* is grown easily and rapidly from seeds. Place some of the orange-red seeds in a waterproof container. Pour some hot water (just about, but not quite, boiling) over the seeds and let them soak for 24 hours. The seeds can then be planted, several to a 6-inch pot or one to a 3-inch pot. Seeds can also be nicked or scarified with a file or clipper to enhance germination. *Wiliwili* can also be grown from fairly large (2 to 6 feet) cuttings.

Fertilize *wiliwili* as you would any plant in the landscape, regularly when the plant is young, in a pot and growing up, and moderately once it is planted in the ground.

LANDSCAPE USE: *Wiliwili* is an attractive tree for the hot, dry, and sunny landscape. More of this native should be grown in our dry lowland gardens. We grow all the alien *Erythrina* from Africa, South America, and Asia, yet rarely do we see our fantastic native member of this genus in any planned public spaces. The new developments in 'Ewa, Kīhei and Kona should include some native *wiliwili* in their landscapes, since it is perfectly adapted after millions of years of flourishing in these same hot places. One drawback with *wiliwili* in the landscape is that it is summer deciduous: it loses its leaves just before it flowers in the summer. If the leafless-with-flowers look is not acceptable, interplant *wiliwili* with evergreen plant material such as *naio*, *mānele*, or *alahe'e*. Non-native evergreen or flowering trees such as plumeria, rainbow shower, and poinciana can also be attractively interplanted with *wiliwili*. Polynesian introductions such as *kou* and *milo* are also good landscape choices.

One of the best places to see *wiliwili* easily is at Koko Crater Botanical Garden. There, an ancient grove still stands, and all the trees are protected by law—Honolulu's famed Exceptional Trees Ordinance, which prevents them from being cut down, bulldozed, or even trimmed without permission. They also grow in Moanalua Gardens, at Ho'omaluhia Botanical Garden, and Waimea Arboretum. There is a group along the Moanalua Freeway by Fort

Hawaiian wiliwili *comes in a range of colors. These orange flowers are found in Kalo'i Gulch in the lower Wai'anae Mountains near Makakilo, O'ahu.*

Wiliwili *with orange and green flowers (and no leaves in the hot dry summer) display their colors in Kona.*

A hapa-haole *planting at Kuilima, on the north shore of O'ahu. Green- and orange-flowered varieties of Hawaiian* wiliwili *are interplanted with Tiare Tahiti, a gardenia from Tahiti, which could just as well be our native gardenia,* nā'ū.

Mānele's *highly ornamental leaves are shiny and feather-shaped.*

Shafter on the makai side of the road. In dry areas like Kīhei and Kona, they still flourish and can be easily seen as you drive along. Dry gulches still grow some *wiliwili*, but fires, sadly too common in dry areas, always destroy these and other native Hawaiian plants. After fires come aggressive weeds that can outcompete *wiliwili* and other natives.

PESTS: Young *wiliwili* are sometimes attacked by a leaf-eating caterpillar. Pick off and destroy these pests, or spray them with insecticidal soap or standard insecticide. The leaves are sometimes attacked by powdery mildew if they are grown in an overly shady place and the leaves get wet frequently. Mature *wiliwili* has few pests.

OTHER USES: *Wiliwili* is naturally pollinated by native Hawaiian birds. Nowadays many birds, both native and introduced, congregate and feed on the pollen and nectar of blossoming trees. The Hawaiians made leis from the attractive blossoms and seeds, and surfboards, canoe outriggers, and net floats from the lightweight, buoyant wood. Hand puppets were carved from the wood, too. We always hear about surfboards of *koa* wood, but lightweight, coastal-growing *wiliwili* was also used a lot. My friend Makana from Ni'ihau told us how he made a surfboard for himself from an old *wiliwili* log. He was known as the best surfer on Ni'ihau, and he ripped on his *wiliwili* board.

MĀNELE, A'E, HAWAIIAN SOAPBERRY

SCIENTIFIC NAME: *Sapindus saponaria*
FAMILY: Sapindaceae (lychee family)

Indigenous to Hawai'i, other Pacific islands, Mexico, South America, and Africa

Mānele is a magnificent tree with shiny green, pinnate leaves. Its rather tiny flowers are followed by seeds that come singly or in pairs. The seeds are covered by a shiny brown, sticky fruit covering. Inside the fruit covering is a round, shiny black seed.

PROPAGATION AND CARE: *Mānele* is best grown from seeds. These should be nicked with a file (scarified) or soaked in hot water for 24 hours to enhance germination.

LANDSCAPE USE: *Mānele* is a tough and good-looking tree. It is adaptable to many climates. Beautiful, majestic specimens grow at the 4,000-foot level near Hawai'i Volcanoes National Park on the Big Island. There are also attractive specimens in one of the toughest conditions for trees—at Ala Moana Beach Park, where it is hot and dry and the water is brackish just inches below the surface, where senseless picnickers sometimes dump hot charcoals at the base of trees, and where mowers and weed trimmers frequently strike trees. The *mānele* is tough, and it thrives there. *Mānele* trees also grow in Moanalua Gardens, at Leilehua High School, and at the Wahiawā Botanical Garden. Bishop Museum has some young, gorgeously shiny-leafed trees around their parking lot.

PESTS: Twig borers sometimes attack the shoots of young *mānele*. Do a preventative bark spray with insecticide, or cut off and throw away the infested wood. Applying standard pesticides will prevent chewing insects from attacking the young growth. Mature trees are fairly tough and pest resistant.

OTHER USES: *Mānele* fruit covering was used as soap. The black seeds inside were polished, a hole was made in them, and then they were strung into leis. The hard wood has seen various uses for construction, utensils, and other purposes.

LONOMEA, ĀULU, KAULU, OʻAHU SOAPBERRY

SCIENTIFIC NAME: *Sapindus oahuensis*
FAMILY: Sapindaceae (lychee family)

Endemic

Lonomea is found only on Oʻahu and Kauaʻi, the older of the main Hawaiian islands. It has large (about 3 by 7 inches), deep green, smooth-textured, pointed leaves. The flowers are somewhat small and insignificant, and they are followed by brown-black fruit. Inside the fruit is a black, oblong seed with a rough texture. *Lonomea* has a striking white trunk. It stands out in the dryland forests where it grows naturally and is handsome in landscapes, for example, when planted against a black or brown moss rock wall. In gardens the trees reach about 30 feet with time. In the wild you sometimes find ancient giants that are 60 feet or more.

PROPAGATION AND CARE: *Lonomea* is grown from seeds. Take the seed out of the fruit and plant it. Fresh seeds germinate readily. You can try scarifying the seeds to speed up the process, but this is not absolutely necessary, as it is with some members of the bean family.

LANDSCAPE USE: As a native of the dry and medium-dry forests, *lonomea* is a tough and less thirsty tree in the landscape. As I mentioned above, its white trunk is handsome and unusual for landscape use. It thrives in tough schoolyards and parks. Two trees grace Ala Moana Beach Park, where they thrive and are green and fruitful, despite difficult conditions.

PESTS: Twig borers sometimes attack the shoots of young *lonomea*. Do a preventative bark spray with insecticide, or cut off and throw

Mānele growing in ideal conditions at Kīpukapuaulu on the Big Island. With a 5000-foot elevation, rich, deep old-volcanic soils, and abundant rain, mānele *can be a gorgeous 60-foot, rounded-canopy forest tree. It is smaller and less majestic in lower elevations and in harsh growing conditions.*

This dryland tree grows along the Honouliuli contour road in the Waiʻanae Mountains of Oʻahu. It thrives in the driest places and is pretty in cultivation, with its striking white trunk and large, deep green leaves. Planting hint: display lonomea *against a black lava rock wall.*

away the infested wood. You can prevent chewing insects from attacking the young growth by applying standard pesticides. Mature trees are fairly tough and pest resistant.

OTHER USES: *Lonomea* smells good enough to eat, but it is not too ono. The seeds were strung into leis.

ALAHE'E

SCIENTIFIC NAME: *Canthium odoratum*
FAMILY: Rubiaceae (gardenia family)

Indigenous to Hawai'i, Micronesia, and the South Pacific from the New Hebrides and New Caledonia east to the Tuamotus

Alahe'e is a shrub or small tree, ranging from 3 to 30 feet tall, with glossy deep green leaves and fragrant clusters of small white blossoms. Fruits are also arranged in attractive clusters, and they turn from a shiny green to a glossy black as they ripen. The bark is white and makes a handsome contrast to the dark shiny leaves and white flowers.

Alahe'e is native to the dryland and moist forests of the Islands. It is not uncommon in the forest. It is tough and drought tolerant in the wild and in landscapes.

PROPAGATION AND CARE: *Alahe'e* can be grown from seeds. Many seeds are produced, but most of them are attacked by a native seed parasite and usually will not grow. The seedlings that do appear grow slowly at first, but take off once established in the ground. This is one of the many native Hawaiian plants for which no foolproof methods of cultivation have been developed. It is worth the effort because of its hardiness and attractive attributes.

Alahe'e has not yet been successfully grown from cuttings or airlayers, but no doubt talented horticulturists will work out the appropriate techniques.

Fertilize young *alahe'e* regularly with organic and slow-release fertilizers incorporated into the potting medium, and also with foliar fertilizer. Plants in the landscape do not need much fertilizer.

LANDSCAPE USE: *Alahe'e* is attractive when grown in its natural form or pruned into a desired shape. It makes an attractive and fragrant specimen shrub, small tree, or hedge. It is tough and drought tolerant once established in the landscape.

One place to see *alahe'e* in cultivation is at the Japanese Garden at the East-West Center on the University of Hawai'i-Mānoa campus. There it is pruned into a dense-leaved shrub in the bonsai style. We grew it at Koko Crater Botanical Garden in the days when we had no irrigation system. It thrived in green perfection even when summers were so hot and dry that the alien grasses and *koa haole* growing around it withered. All the same, it is more healthy and attractive with water.

Clusters of small, fragrant white flowers appear on alahe'e *several times a year.*

My husband, Clark, found this bonsai specimen of alahe'e *at the Japanese garden at the East-West Center, UH-Mānoa. This is a creative trimming of a tough and versatile native plant—true horticulture with natives!*

PESTS: Developing seeds are attacked by the plume moth. Spraying the seeds on the parent tree with standard insecticide, as they are ripening, can prevent this problem.

Young leaves and new growth, if overfertilized with high nitrogen fertilizers, or grown in too shady a spot, are attacked by sucking insects like aphids and scales, which are carried to the plant and protected by ants. Treat these with insecticidal soap or standard insecticides and ant baits.

OTHER USES: *Alahe'e* has very hard wood with a straight grain. The wood was used for *'ō'ō* (digging sticks) and spears.

The name *alahe'e* is an example of the poetry of the Hawaiian language. *Ala* means fragrant and *he'e* means octopus, or slippery like an octopus. *Alahe'e* has blossoms that you can stick your nose into and smell, but they are better enjoyed in the patient Hawaiian style, by letting the breeze waft the scent to you. The Hawaiians expressed all this as a "slippery fragrance."

Wayne Takeuchi does the non-Hawaiian thing and inhales deeply of the subtle perfume of alahe'e *at Ho'omaluhia Botanical Garden.*

HŌ'AWA

SCIENTIFIC NAME: *Pittosporum* spp.
FAMILY: Pittosporaceae (Pittosporum family)

Endemic (10 species)
Naturalized (2 species)

Hō'awa is a small to medium tree with attractive and interesting leaves. Quite often the leaves are copper colored from dense fuzzy hairs on the lower surface. *Hō'awa* flowers are creamy white, with short stems and a light fragrance. The fruit are rough textured, grow close to the stem, and are striking when they ripen and split open. On ripening, the inner orange fruit with shiny black seeds is revealed. *Hō'awa* includes ten endemic species.

PROPAGATION AND CARE: *Ho'awa* can be grown from seeds or cuttings.

LANDSCAPE USE: *Hō'awa* is a nice small to medium tree or large shrub for the landscape. The leaves and fruit give it an ornamental look. It is tough and somewhat drought tolerant.

PESTS: *Hō'awa* has few pests.

OTHER USES: *Hō'awa* seeds are one of the favorite foods of the *'alalā*, our rare native Hawaiian crow. The outer fruit was used medicinally by the ancient Hawaiians, who pounded up the outer layer of the fruit valves and applied it to sores.

Native plant lover Ray Tabata of U.H. Sea Grant admires this hō'awa *growing at the Bishop Museum.*

This handsome mature koa *grows on Kaua'i.*

As the koa *tree matures, it loses the true (small, feather-shaped) leaves and grows phyllodes, flattened leaf stems that serve as leaves.*

KOA

SCIENTIFIC NAME: *Acacia koa*
FAMILY: Fabaceae (bean family)

Endemic

Koa is a large, majestic tree of the Hawaiian forest. It grows from 15 to 50 feet tall, or even larger under ideal conditions and with many years of growth. It has an attractive, rounded shape and sickle-shaped, gray-green "leaves," small yellow powder puff flowers, and brown seed pods. The new-moon-shaped "leaves" are actually flattened leaf stems, full of chlorophyll, and are called phyllodes. They are the result of evolution during much drier times; phyllodes lose less water to hot dry air than leaves do. True leaves, which are light green and feather shaped, are found on young trees and sometimes on branches that have been wounded or overly shaded. The bark is gray and smooth on young trees and deeply furrowed longitudinally on mature trees.

When the Polynesians discovered these islands, there were large *koa* groves growing with other trees and plants in the forest. Because it was such a tall, magnificent tree they named it *koa*, "the warrior."

PROPAGATION AND CARE: *Koa* is grown from seeds. Like other members of the bean family, it will sprout better after a 24-hour soak in water that was initially almost boiling.

LANDSCAPE USE: *Koa* makes a lovely tree in the large-scale landscape. It is obviously one of the prime candidates for reforestation and should be considered strongly as an alternate crop to sugar, and certainly to the low-value eucalyptus. It deserves to be more widely grown. It is not as huge as people might think and, as I tell my dad, if it gets too big for your yard, cut it down and make a surfboard (or a dining set, or a fine calabash, or whatever you want out of the fine, highly prized wood).

At higher elevations the trees grow large and have fine, straight trunks. They also have fewer pests and diseases at upper elevations. The ideal elevational range is between 1,500 and 4,000 feet, but *koa* will also grow at sea level. We grew it at the Honolulu Zoo in a large sewer pipe filled with well-aged elephant manure and good soil. We also grow it at the Hale Koa Hotel in well-amended soil with a good irrigation system, but it is adapted to and grows better at higher elevations.

PESTS: The tree should be kept in good health and monitored for insects. The trunk and stems are sometimes attacked by coffee twig borers and black twig borers, which are accompanied by galleries of wood-rotting fungus. A preventative bark spray with a systemic insecticide like Dursban or Sevin and removal of all infested branches should keep the tree pest free. Cut off any insect-infested wood and **throw it away** so the insects won't fly around and infest other plants.

OTHER USES: The wood is valuable and prized by woodworkers around the world. Some people call the wood "Hawaiian mahogany," and it does resemble mahogany with its deep red-brown color and wavy wood grain. It is said that it takes 100 years to grow a marketable tree, but with proper diligent horticulture and ideal elevation, soil, and other growing conditions, wood-producing trees may be grown more rapidly. The wood is now used for prized ukuleles, furniture, fine cabinetry, and woodworking. It was used by the early Hawaiians for many things: war canoes and surfboards, canoe paddles, weapons, tools, and non-poi calabashes (if *koa* is used to serve poi, it is said to give the food a bitter taste because of the tannins in the wood). The bark was used to make a red kapa dye.

The upland forests of Maui and the Big Island are probably where huge trees for large war canoes came from. Control of these forests by Kamehameha on the Big Island and Kahekili of Maui must have aided their victories over *ali'i* from lower-elevation islands. Many rituals and religious ceremonies accompanied the cutting of a *koa* tree and fashioning it into a canoe. The god Kū and the *ali'i* had to be formally petitioned for permission to cut the tree. After it was cut, the *kahuna kālaiwa'a* (a priest specializing in the rituals of canoe making) watched closely for the insect-eating forest bird *'elepaio*, one of the forms of the goddess Le'a, wife of Kū. *'Elepaio* are curious birds and would certainly come to investigate a major disturbance in the forest like the felling of a giant *koa*. If the *'elepaio* landed on the *koa* log and pecked at it, the *kahuna* gave it back to the forest, having been warned that the *koa* log was insect infested.

The mast in Hawaiian canoes was made from a *koa* trunk or large branch, about 5 to 6 inches in diameter.

Koa *blossoms look like small, fuzzy yellow pompoms. Long brown bean pods follow the pollinated flowers. These pods can grow new* koa *trees and restore our Hawaiian forests.* Koa *is one of our most prized Hawaiian trees and we should grow it all over—in gardens in our forests and as a high-quality timber crop. Foresters and horticulturists are now saying 30 years of growth in ideal conditions will produce some prime hardwood. One hundred years of growth is said to be required for the highest-quality* koa.

KOAI'A OR *KOAI'E*

SCIENTIFIC NAME: *Acacia koaia*
FAMILY: Fabaceae (bean family)

Endemic

Koai'a is a small tree, 15 to 25 feet tall, from the dry leeward areas of Kaua'i, Maui, Moloka'i, Lāna'i and Hawai'i. It is related to true Hawaiian *koa* but is smaller and more adapted to dry conditions. It has an attractive rounded shape and sickle-shaped, gray-green "leaves," small yellow powder puff flowers, and brown seed pods.

PROPAGATION AND CARE: *Koai'a* is grown from seeds. Like other members of the bean family, it will sprout better after a 24-hour soak in water that was initially almost boiling.

LANDSCAPE USE: *Koai'a* makes a lovely tree in the landscape. It deserves to be more widely grown. It is not a huge tree like *koa* and is therefore more suitable for the average landscape. It thrives in dryland forests and is suitable for the xeriscape garden.

Koai'a *growing at a* keiki *community park in Waimea on the Big Island. Note the stiff, short, silvered phyllodes of this rare* koa *"cousin."*

PESTS: The tree should be kept in good health and monitored for insects. The trunk and stems are sometimes attacked by coffee twig borers and black twig borers. A preventative bark spray with a systemic insecticide like Dursban or Sevin and removal of all infested branches should keep the tree pest free. Cut off any insect-infested wood and **throw it away** so the insects won't fly around and infest other plants.

OTHER USES: The wood is hard and dense. In the past, when it was more abundant, it was favored for making long-lasting fence posts for pastures. Many of these old fence posts are still in use in Kohala. The early Hawaiians probably used it for tools and weapons. Its hard, dense nature made it suitable for carved fishhooks as well.

Koaiʻa is a beautiful small to medium-sized tree with hard wood that thrives in drier, lower elevation areas better than koa does. This tree is growing along the upper Kohala road on the Big Island.

ʻŌHIʻA LEHUA

SCIENTIFIC NAME: *Metrosideros polymorpha*
FAMILY: Myrtaceae (myrtle family)

Endemic

From high, cloud-drenched forests, to salt-misted windward coastal slopes, to freshly cooled lava beds, the *ʻōhiʻa lehua* is found. It is an extremely variable Hawaiian plant. It can be a tree, a shrub, or a prostrate bog dweller. It ranges from a tall, majestic tree to a low, ground-hugging shrub. It ranges in height from a few inches to 100 feet tall, depending on habitat and variety. The usual flower color is red, but it also ranges to orange, salmon, yellow, and almost white. The leaves (new leaf tips are called *liko*) can be glabrous (shiny) or tomentose (hairy), and green, reddish, and even purple or gray. The *liko* are often the most vibrantly colored and textured of leaves.

ʻŌhiʻa is a fairly common plant in the Hawaiian rain forest. It can also be found near the coast in wet areas like Wailau on Molokaʻi and Puna on the Big Island. It used to be found more widely all over the Hawaiian Islands, but because of development, competition from introduced plants and insects, and overpicking, its range has become reduced. It is generally considered to be a rain forest plant, but some types do well on the coast and tolerate salt spray. It does not seem to be a drought-tolerant plant.

Orange- (top) and golden-flowered varieities of ʻōhiʻa lehua at Hoʻomaluhia Botanical Garden. This collection of choice varieties was inspired by the gardening efforts of Jimmy and Nellie Pang.

PROPAGATION AND CARE: Today, responding to consumer demand, we are finding more commercial nurseries growing ʻōhiʻa from seed, cuttings, or air-layers. You can buy a healthy plant and continue to grow it yourself.

Seeds are the best method for the home gardener. Growing by cuttings or air-layers is better left to a professional with specialized tools and techniques, who will grow them from cultivated sources and not destroy the ones growing in the wild.

Seeds: Growing ʻōhiʻa lehua from seeds is the simplest method, but it is nonetheless fun and challenging. The seedlings become like precious *keiki*. Collect fresh seed capsules. *Ōhiʻa lehua* has tiny seeds about 1/16 inch long and the width and color of baby-fine blond hair. These seeds are easy to grow if collected fresh and not water soaked. Sprinkle the tiny seeds onto firm, moist potting medium. The ingredient they most require is water, which they need daily for the first year of their lives. Water daily and transplant into individual pots when the seedlings have two sets of leaves. With daily watering and monthly foliar fertilizing, a 2-foot plant can be produced in one year.

Purple ʻōhiʻa lehua *with flowers and seed capsules forming*

The flowers are a mass of color, thanks mainly to the stamens (male flowers). After the flower is pollinated, the stamens fall and the calyx (the green, cup-shaped receptacle below the stamens) begins to swell and turn brown. When the seeds are ripe, the calyx splits, and in nature the seeds spill out with every passing gust of the trade winds. Landing on a suitable growing medium (like a *hāpuʻu* tree fern trunk), and given adequate moisture, the tiny seeds will start growing, eventually sending roots down to the ground and some day becoming gorgeous trees or shrubs, depending on the growing conditions.

To grow *ʻōhiʻa lehua* yourself, think of how the plant thrives in the wild. The tiny seeds are somewhat vulnerable, but this is simply remedied. Use sterile potting soil, not dirt, for the seeds. This can be peat moss and perlite or sponge rock, *hāpuʻu*, black cinder, vermiculite, or whatever you prefer. Put the planting medium in a clean pot. Water it and firm it down with another pot of the same size. The potting medium should be about an inch below the rim of the pot. Sprinkle the tiny seeds on top, do not cover them, and then water **gently**—like a misting rain—so as to not wash away the tiny seeds, and water at least daily. You can put the base of the pot in a saucer to help ensure a continuous supply of moisture. You can also grow them indoors in a covered, clear container. Do not let it overheat or the seeds will cook. When the seedlings have two sets of leaves or are about 1 inch tall, transplant them into individual pots with rich organic soil that drains well. Watch for insects and disease and use standard insecticides or fungicides, at half strength. When they are 6 to 12 inches tall and appear strong and vigorous, they can be planted in the ground or in a larger pot.

Like the blossoms, the liko, *or young leaves, prized for lei making, come in a wide variety of colors, shapes, sizes, and textures.*

To plant them in the ground, first dig and loosen the soil. You can just add some slow-release fertilizer, or you can add soil conditioners to the planting mixture. Add well-rotted compost, black cinders, and *hāpuʻu*. Use a slow-release fertilizer like Complehumus 8–8–8 or Osmocote. Water well and daily if it doesn't rain heavily (at least an hour of rain). The hole should be twice as wide as the pot. You can fertilize with foliar fertilizer once or twice a month or use a very dilute solution when you water.

If you are planning to keep the *ʻōhiʻa lehua* in a pot, move it up to the next pot one size at a time—that is, don't transplant from a small pot to a giant one. You might think you're saving time, but the plant could "drown" in too large a pot and die.

Air-layers can be made, but this is best done on cultivated plants,

The red of this 'ōhi'a lehua at Mt. Ka'ala, O'ahu, is the classic lehua flower color, beautiful in the wild or in a well-watered garden.

so as not to harm the plants in the wild. Standard air-layering practices can be followed, but a fairly strong rooting hormone such as a 10% solution of Dip-N-Gro is recommended. Some trees are more easily propagated by air-layering than others. Aerial roots on the parent plant are one indication of easier air-layering.

To grow 'ōhi'a from cuttings, a mist system is usually required. If you are home to water several times a day, or if you live in the rain forest, you may be able to grow 'ōhi'a cuttings without a mist system. Mist, coupled with a 10% solution of Dip-N-Gro rooting hormone, is beneficial. Select wood that is about as thick as a pencil (1/4 inch in diameter) and 4 to 6 inches long. Tip and stem cuttings with healthy leaves are best. Cut the leaves in half and remove leaves from the lower inch of the cutting. Dip the cutting into the hormone solution for 10 seconds.

Good rooting media for 'ōhi'a cuttings include equal parts perlite and vermiculite; 2 parts perlite peat moss to 1 part pure vermiculate; and pure perlite. This depends on the grower's climate and preference. Success of rooting, like air-layers, depends a great deal on the parent plant. Experienced growers like Marie MacDonald have found that some plants will produce 100% rooted cuttings while others are nearly impossible to reproduce this way.

'Ōhi'a lehua responds well to fertilizer. Slow-release, organic, or foliar fertilizers are best. Foliar is best applied one or two times a month. Follow the label directions for organic or slow-release forms.

LANDSCAPE USE: *'Ōhi'a lehua* is beautiful in the landscape, as a blooming tree or shrub in the ground or in a large pot. A good planting medium for potted 'ōhi'a is a mixture of equal parts peat moss, perlite, and cinder. In Wahiawā, Mānoa, and Waimea on the Big Island, people are growing them in their home and business landscapes. As propagation and maintenance techniques are worked out, we should see more 'ōhi'a lehua in landscapes.

One important note, especially during establishment in the ground, or if the plants are to be kept in containers, is to **never let them dry out**. Daily watering is essential in areas that do not receive daily rainfall. You should plan on this daily watering for at least four years to get the plant fully established in the ground.

PESTS: Rose beetles sometimes damage the leaves. These can be handled with standard insecticides. Sometimes 'ōhi'a is attacked by nematodes or root-rotting fungi. For the home gardener, one of the best prevention techniques for nematodes is addition of lots of organic matter to the soil to keep the plants growing vigorously. Clandosan is a fairly new product, found in local garden stores, that will help combat the ravages of nematodes. It is a shellfish by-product. By incorporating Clandosan into the growing medium, you help nourish the beneficial microorganisms. These "good microbes" eat nematode eggs, thereby reducing the nematode population and improving the health of your plant. Perfect drainage is important to prevent fungal attacks. Subdue or Truban fungicides as a soil drench will help prevent root rot.

'Ōhi'a, along with mosses and ferns, is one of the few plants to grow on lava, converting it gradually to soil and making habitats for other more fragile plants. This 'ōhi'a is growing in new pāhoehoe lava.

OTHER USES: 'Ōhi'a lehua is one of the most beautiful, beloved, and legendary of native Hawaiian plants. Its blossoms and young leaf tips are highly prized for leis; this is a good reason to grow 'ōhi'a more widely. The trees, especially those near accessible trails, are becoming stripped in the wild. Trees suffer dieback from overpicking. Lei makers should cultivate plants in their own gardens and help to protect the plants in the wild.

However you grow it, 'ōhi'a is a beautiful addition to a garden and something you rarely see today. It is nice as a tree or shrub and is beautiful in leis, flower arrangements (fresh and dried), or as a flower in your hair.

There are many Hawaiian legends and proverbs about 'ōhi'a lehua. It is one of the five plants sacred to Laka, goddess of the hula. Hālau hula and others who cherish lei 'ōhi'a lehua should grow the plants in gardens for their special occasions and events.

LOULU

SCIENTIFIC NAME: Pritchardia spp.
FAMILY: Arecaceae (palm family)

Endemic

We have many kinds of palms gracing our landscapes here in the islands. But only one palm genus, Pritchardia, is native, and though it contains quite a few species, none of them are common these days. To the ancient Hawaiians, these were all known as loulu. They have broad, fan-shaped leaves and no thorns. The flowers are golden yellow and are followed by fruit. Fruit size, shape, and color vary by species.

Fossil pollen evidence indicates that loulu used to be quite widespread in many parts of the islands. Salt Lake was filled with them and that lei and dye maker's favorite, 'a'ali'i.

As with many native plants (wiliwili and 'ōhi'a lehua being other prime examples), it seems that we grow the foreign cousins much more than we do the native Hawaiians. In this case, we grow the Pritchardia species from Fiji and Tahiti much more than we do our unique Hawaiian plants.

There are types of loulu unique to each of the Hawaiian islands, much as there are with our native hibiscus. Some islands have more than one type, and each is unique to a mountain, valley, or particular area on that island or mountain. To keep things from getting too mixed up and hybridized, we should try to grow the species that is native to our area. It will thrive the best there, because it is adapted—after millions of years, you would be too!

On O'ahu our main loulu is Pritchardia martii. It is native to the Ko'olaus. It has fruit the size of golf balls. Mature palms have silvery leaf undersides.

On Moloka'i the common one is the loulu lelo, Pritchardia hillebrandii. The undersides of the leaves are silvery, and the fruit is black and marble-sized. You can see a hundred-year-old specimen of loulu lelo growing in the nēnē exhibit at the Honolulu Zoo. This

Lehua mamo, or yellow 'ōhi'a lehua, grown from seeds at Ho'omaluhia and set against a gorgeous natural backdrop of uluhe, the land-healing fern. This is where we found out that 'ōhi'a lehua in gardens need daily watering to survive.

The undersides of loulu fronds are gorgeous, with fine silvery or golden hairs lighting up the whole tree. Notice the blooming flower cluster.

particular tree is protected by law (Honolulu's Exceptional Trees Ordinance). There is another species from Moloka'i that is so rare there is only one tree left in the wild. This is P. *munroi*, named after that great saver of native plants and forests George Munro, of Lāna'i forest and watershed protection fame. There are quite a few specimens of this species growing well in botanical gardens. One day—with care, protection from rats, and nurturing—more plants may be grown to be replanted in the wild on Moloka'i.

The dry and salty lowlands on the Kona side of the Big Island have a gorgeous *loulu, Pritchardia affinis.*

Ni'ihau has its own unique type, and so does the islet of Nihoa, northwest of Ni'ihau. Ni'ihau has the extremely rare *Pritchardia aylmer-robinsonii.* The Nihoa *loulu* is known appropriately as *Pritchardia remota.* It has golden undersides on its leaves and it is very handsome.

PROPAGATION AND CARE: *Loulu* palms are not hard to grow if you can get mature seeds. Unfortunately, in its wild home there are many introduced animals that prey on seeds and seedlings. Rats love to eat the seeds while still on the tree and also on the ground. Pigs and goats eat the seeds and seedlings, so you don't see many young *loulu* in the forests today. Weeds also can easily outcompete them, and wildfires burn up the palms and their seeds.

Once you get good seeds though, take off the outer husk and bury the seeds half-way in a pot of clean, well-drained potting soil. Water daily, and in a few months (all palms take a while) the seedling will pop up. Grow it until it's about a foot tall, and then plant it in the ground or in a series of ever larger pots.

Many botanical gardens and private collectors grow *loulu* palms. If many species are grown in the same vicinity, the seeds could become hybridized. The way to get a pure species from a collection like this is to hand-pollinate the flowers and then bag them to prevent cross-pollination.

LANDSCAPE USE: *Loulu* are gorgeous in the landscape and deserve to be much more widely grown. You can plant a whole grove or have a specimen *loulu*. They can grow in a big pot for several years, but eventually they should be planted in the ground.

PESTS: The main pests of *loulu* are mentioned above. Mealy bugs sometimes attack the young, growing roots. Keep these adventitious roots (which grow out from the base of the trunk) well covered with soil or potting medium. You can kill the mealy bugs with a standard garden insecticide or insecticidal soap applied as a drench to the medium.

OTHER USES: Beautiful *pāpale* (hats) were once woven from *loulu* fronds. The fruit, *hāwane*, can be peeled and eaten. It tastes something like coconut.

This sea stack, an eroded remnant of Moloka'i, is home to the last loulu *palm forest, protected from alien grazing animals like the numerous goats, deer, and pigs that devastate native plants on the main island. Ancient pollen sediment core samples collected from Salt Lake and Kawainui marshes on O'ahu show that three of the most common plants in ancient Hawai'i were* 'a'ali'i, loulu, *and* kanaloa *(a plant unknown to modern science until recently discovered on a sea stack off Kaho'olawe by Steve Perlman). Photo by Steve Perlman, courtesy of the National Tropical Botanical Garden.*

Clark Leavitt admires a native planting of loulu *palms and* 'uki'uki, *or* Dianella, *the blue-flowered and -fruited native lily at Waimea Botanical Garden (now the Waimea Valley Audubon Center).*

LAMA, ELAMA, HAWAIIAN EBONY

SCIENTIFIC NAME: *Diospyros sandwicensis; D. hillebrandii*
FAMILY: Ebenaceae (ebony family)

Endemic

Lama is a tree of the dry and moderately wet (mesic) forests of Hawai'i. The early Hawaiians cherished and found many uses for it. One of the most beautiful uses for *lama* takes advantage of its hard and attractive wood, as suggested by one of the Western names for *lama*, Hawaiian ebony. In fact, *lama* is related to the valuable ebony and also looks like it. The outer wood is black and can take a high polish. The sapwood is white, and the heartwood is reddish-brown with areas of yellow or deeper red. This is yet another native Hawaiian tree that I would recommend planting for those of us who want to see alternate, long-lasting, 'āina-friendly industries like tree growing and fine woodworking in Hawai'i.

Lama is known scientifically as *Diospyros sandwicensis*. There is also another rare species of *lama*, *D. hillebrandii*, found only on O'ahu and Kaua'i, the older of the main Hawaiian islands; it is also called *elama*.

If you know how and where to look in our forests, you will see that *lama* is not all that rare—but if we don't take care, it will become so. For example, when we first used to hike in North Hālawa Valley there were quite a few *lama* in the lower valley. When the bulldozers for H-3 came through, the forest was ripped open and the *lama* started to die. Not knowing what these valuable trees were, we bulldozed them into the mud—the wood wasn't even saved. We should all educate ourselves so mistakes and waste don't continue.

This lama *growing in the dryland forest at Kanepu'u on Lāna'i has yellow or orange fruit when ripe. (The O'ahu variety usually has red fruit.)* Lama *are easy to grow from seeds: pop the seeds out of the fruit and plant them in a pot. Water daily.*

PROPAGATION AND CARE: If ripe, fresh seeds can be found, they are easy to sprout and grow. Squeeze the seed (or seeds; some fruit have up to four seeds inside) onto moist, firm medium in a clean pot. Cover with about 1/4 inch of potting medium and water regularly. Like many Hawaiian plants, *lama* is trickier and slower growing as time goes on. It has to be carefully nurtured once planted in the ground. *Lama* needs certain mauka forest soils to thrive. This is not one that you can plant in beach sand.

LANDSCAPE USE: Besides being an important part of our forests and a valuable hardwood, *lama* is a beautiful shrub or tree. The trunks are black and straight, the leaves are deep green, and the new leaves come out pink or red. The fruits, which often appear around Christmas, are bright and ornamental.

PESTS: Twig borers sometimes attack *lama*. Spray the trunk with insecticide twice a year to prevent infestation. Scale insects sometimes attack the young growth if too much fertilizer is applied.

OTHER USES: *Lama* is one of the plants of Laka, goddess of hula. The white part of the wood was placed on hula altars to symbolize

Liko, *or new red leaves, of* lama, *growing in a nursery at Wahiawā, show another attractive asset of our native ebony, or persimmon.*

and pay respect to Laka and also to fence in sacred enclosures. The place name Kapalama means enlightenment (*lama*) fence (*kapa*); there was a school for *ali'i* keiki there in times of old.

A familiar relative of *lama* is the oriental persimmon, or *kaki*, also in the Ebenaceae family. *Lama* has a small fruit, about an inch long and half an inch wide. The fruit is either yellow, orange, or red when ripe. It is edible but not as ono to people as a persimmon. It is ono to native Hawaiian birds, which ate and then "planted" the seeds for millions of years before people came. Today many of these birds are extinct or rare, the lands have been altered by people, and there are fewer *lama* trees.

Lama is a dominant tree at the Kānepu'u dryland forest on Lāna'i. Concerned Lāna'i citizens, among them Carol Ah Toong, "Uncle" Sol Kaopuiki, and newly elected councilman Sol Kaho'ohalahala, have been quietly protecting and nurturing the vulnerable forest for years. The Nature Conservancy of Hawai'i manages and protects this forest. Alien grazing animals like axis deer (imported from India) and mouflon sheep must be kept out of the forest. They munch the trees, devour the seedlings, and even rub antlers on the trunks to girdle and kill *lama* and other Hawaiian plants. Without the birds to eat and spread the seeds, they must be carefully collected, grown in the nursery, and replanted into the forest. With *lama*, at least, once the deer are fenced out, many trees come back on their own. At Kānepu'u, *lama* and *olopua*, the native olive, are the most common native plants.

'ILIAHI, SANDALWOOD

SCIENTIFIC NAME: *Santalum freycinetianum* and S. *pyrularium*
FAMILY: Santalaceae (sandalwood family)

Endemic

'Iliahi, or Hawaiian sandalwood, has droopy-looking, slender, usually gray-green leaves. The flowers are about 1/4-inch wide and have four star-shaped cream or red petals. The fruit are about the size of a small olive and are reddish or purplish when ripe. They have a thin outer layer of pulp with a hard seed inside, shaped like the fruit. Native birds find this a tasty and rewarding seed to eat and thereby spread *'iliahi* in the wild.

We also have a coastal type of sandalwood: *'iliahialo'e* (S. *ellipticum*). It grows near the beach and in dry lowland forests. It is known in Latin as *Santalum*. Our native Hawaiian species are *Santalum freycinetianum* and S. *pyrularium*. They are in the Santalaceae family. They have also have a rare Hawaiian relative called *hulu moa*.

Different types of sandalwood grow in other tropical places like Indonesia, Australia, Nepal, and India. Industries harvest the wood in these places, and in Australia an edible crop is made from the fruit. This inspired me to try a taste of ours—

This is the flower of the rare Lāna'i variety of sandalwood.

not too 'ono, but okay. It also crossed my mind that being eaten by a bird might aid the seed in sprouting. I chewed on the pulp and hard seeds for a while and then planted the seeds. It didn't seem to help germination much—some sprouted, most didn't.

You can see 'iliahi if you hike on trails in the medium and wet forests on all the islands. Once you know what to look for, you will see it growing here and there. You seldom, if ever, though, see seedlings growing in the forests. Although you'll see that the trees are fairly common, it is always a happy reward when you spot one. Most people who know something about native Hawaiian forest plants will be able to teach you to spot 'iliahi. Such groups as the Sierra Club, Hawai'i Trail and Mountain Club, and Moanalua Gardens Foundation sponsor and lead educational hikes on various islands.

The droopy, wilted-looking leaves of this O'ahu 'iliahi *are a way to identify it in the forest. There are a fair number of* 'iliahi *along the popular* 'Aiea ridge trail on O'ahu.

PROPAGATION AND CARE: *'Iliahi* are not easy to grow. I've been trying for over twenty years, with hundreds of seeds, and have only a few living plants today to show for all that effort. Still, I keep trying and so do lots of other Hawai'i growers. Bob Hirano of Lyon Arboretum, Richard Nakagawa of the State Forestry Department on Maui, and Dr. K.B. Chun are some fellow 'iliahi growers who have had more success than I have had.

First, it is often hard to find seeds; then they take a while to sprout and only a few do so. Once you do get a seedling to grow, it has certain "mysterious requirements" for continued growth. 'Iliahi have special structures on their roots called haustoria. 'Iliahi is a semi-parasitic plant, and it uses the haustoria to latch onto nearby plants' roots and "borrow" some water and nutrients from them. Many kinds of plants have been used as companion plants for 'iliahi. Some research shows that you should start with a fibrous rooted plant (best results were from that noxious weed the spiny amaranth) and then plant it next to a tree host as it matures. Ironwood, strawberry guava, mock orange, and coffee have been good hosts, and native Hawaiian *koa*, *māmane* and hibiscus work too. With time in the ground, the seedlings latch on a bit to all the plants around them. Because of this, you should never pull out weeds around an 'iliahi. Cutting the weeds is okay, because the roots are left intact. Some researchers think that it is possible to supply the needed mystery ingredient with nutrients and fertilizers. Obviously, this is just one of many native Hawaiian plants that cry out for more people to experiment with growing them and to find out what they need to grow and thrive.

'Iliahi a lo'e, or coastal sandalwood, S. ellipticum, *shows its attractive leaf form near Makapu'u on O'ahu.*

LANDSCAPE USE: We don't know enough about how to grow 'iliahi to freely recommend it for the landscape, but with time and good Hawaiian horticulture this should change. You can see both the native Hawaiian and imported Indian sandalwood at Foster Botanical Gardens. We grew the native with a mock orange as the companion plant.

OTHER USES: I get a lot of questions about sandalwood. Many people are interested in growing this important Hawaiian plant.

Luscious fruiting head of iliahi *at Kānepuʻu, Lānaʻi. This is a happy sight for rare plant horticulturists: ripe fruit of a very rare form of native sandalwood, ready to be propagated carefully in the nursery.*

ʻOhe makai, with leaves and young fruit. A wet winter on Lānaʻi helped produce an abundant crop of attractive, glossy fruit heads filled with seeds at the Kānepuʻu Dryland Forest Preserve.

The author carefully harvesting fruit of ʻohe makai *later in the summer. In the hot, dry months, the leaves fall, conserving moisture. Photo by Jennifer Higashino.*

ʻIliahi is so tied to our past, to the human history of using the forests and forest materials.

Even though ʻiliahi was ruthlessly harvested in the past, to the detriment of the forests and the Hawaiian people, it is not all that rare in the forest today. If you know where and how to look, you can see it. Some types, such as the Lānaʻi variety, are very rare. Only a few plants grow there today, and every feral imported grazing animal running loose lessens the numbers. Axis deer and mouflon sheep on Lānaʻi not only munch the native plants but wear away the soil and cause it to wash into the ocean, killing the reef and muddying the waters.

ʻOHE MAKAI, ʻOHE KUKULUAEʻO, ʻOHE, ʻOHEʻOHE (ON NIʻIHAU), ʻOHEOKAI

SCIENTIFIC NAME: *Reynoldsia sandwicensis*
FAMILY: Araliaceae

Indigenous

ʻOhe makai is a plant cousin of *Munroidendron*. It is a tree of dryland forests. The dryland forests of Kānepuʻu on Lānaʻi have a fair abundance of ʻohe makai, including one gigantic gnarled specimen that is well-beloved and revered by Hawaiian people and plant lovers. There are *moʻolelo* about the ʻohe makai of Lānaʻi and Molokaʻi. One tragic love story features this tree.

Ironically, George Munro helped to save this tree and the forests of Lānaʻi at the same time he managed the cattle ranching operation. He and his *paniolo* eliminated pigs on the island, fenced off native forests from the destructive, forest-ravaging cattle, mouflon sheep, and axis deer, and planted windbreaks and Norfolk pines to catch more water and fog drip for this low, dry island, which is in the rain shadow of Maui and Haleakalā.

ʻOhe makai is summer deciduous; like *wiliwili* (*Erythrina sandwicensis*) and other native Hawaiian dry forest trees, it sheds leaves to conserve moisture and display its flowers for pollinators in the summer and regreens in the wet months. It also has a large, fat moisture-holding trunk to help it survive the dry times.

LANDSCAPE USE: ʻOhe makai is an ideal tree for xeriscape gardens or any gardens in hot, dry areas. Its unique appearance will jazz up the garden of the jaded. The robust, whitish trunk is attractive set against a dark backdrop like a moss rock wall. Each tree grows in a twisty, gnarled style all its own. We come to recognize individual trees in the wild by their shape, size, and growth habit. These are good features to capitalize on in a landscape.

Protect the trunk from mechanical damage from line trimmers and other tools. A nice mulch dish of red or black cinders will benefit the tree and highlight its good looks.

Tetraplasandra is another native member of this family. It is a tree of mesic and rain forests. It is also handsome in the landscape and grows taller than *Reynoldsia*. Nice mature specimen trees, dating from the 1970s, can be seen at Wahiawā Botanical Garden, and Hoʻomaluhia Botanical Garden has trees that are about 20 years old.

PROPAGATION: Grow *Reynoldsia* from fresh ripe seeds. The fruits are black and shiny and soft when ripe. Clean the fruit pulp off the seeds, soak them in warm water for 24 hours, and then plant them in a clean pot of sterile media. Monitor the vulnerable seedlings diligently. The tree is pretty tough once mature.

PESTS: Grow *ʻohe makai* is a sunny spot with well-drained soil and keep an eye on it. Underfertilize and watch for and treat the usual garden insect pests.

OTHER USES: The tree produces a yellow resin that was used in old Hawaiʻi. Hawaiians made stilts from the soft wood of this plant, and it gets its name from the *aeʻo*, the Hawaiian stilt bird. This play on words is also an example of the Hawaiian concept of "*kinolau*," or the different body forms taken on by supernatural beings.

HALA PEPE, LEʻIE

SCIENTIFIC NAME: *Pleomele* spp.
FAMILY: Agavaceae

Endemic

Hala pepe is a beautiful and meaningful native Hawaiian plant that is not common today. There are 6 Hawaiian species; some are fairly common and most are rare and slow growing. When you first see one, you might think it looks like a pointy-leaf ti plant or a more subtly colored money tree. Look more closely and your eyes and other senses will tell you that this is a unique native Hawaiian plant. You also might think that it would be a nice addition to your garden.

You are right; *hala pepe* would be gorgeous in gardens, and lovely as choice potted specimen plants, but they are not that easy to get started. They also grow very slowly, compared with their nonnative relatives like ti leaves and money trees. It is particularly hard to find them on Oʻahu, and when you do, their beauty and the fact that they are still growing here makes you feel happy and hopeful.

In some forests they are fairly common. I remember tramping over the *ʻaʻā* in a Kona *waena* forest with landscape architect Brenda Lam. A new road had been cut through these dry, mostly native forest lands. This road opened the area up. This provides access for those, like us, who want to look at and enjoy the plants, but it also brings in weeds if we're not careful.

Fire, also, is a killer of native Hawaiian plants and their seeds. Roads can mean fires, a careless cigarette butt or ill-timed backfire igniting the alien dry weeds and grasses that inevitably line roads and burn hot, killing our precious native plants and their seeds.

Hala pepe is one of many native plants that we should take the

Fruit head, or infrutescence, of ʻohe makai, harvested at maturity and ready for the fruit to be soaked off in warm water and the precious seeds planted and nurtured in the nursery.

Hala pepe *in bloom—what a gorgeous and rare sight, a lei makers' delight! The flowers provide pollen and nectar for native bird and insect pollinators. This is a plant with abundant potential for lei makers' and bird lovers' gardens. Photo by Jean Cote.*

time and energy to learn about, grow, and nurture both in our gardens and in the wild wonderful places where it still grows.

OTHER USES: *Hala pepe*, along with *maile, palapalai, 'ōhi'a lehua*, and *'ie'ie (Freycineta arborea)*, is one of the plants of Laka, goddess of the hula. It is a precious and revered plant, but sometimes this reverence does the plants no good. We must all be conscious of how we use and abuse native Hawaiian plants. One case of abuse made me heartsick at what should have been a happy and memorable occasion. I had won tickets on the radio for the 30th-anniversary concert of a popular Hawaiian group and their *hālau*. I had loved these guys for years and enjoyed many of their performances and have their albums and tapes. The concert was at the fabulous Hawaii Theatre, another restored piece of Hawaiiana. All the sacred Hawaiian plants of Laka were up on stage. I was disheartened to see that there were several HUGE *hala pepe* cuttings. *How many years had they been growing in the forest before being whacked for a two-day concert?* I thought sadly. (The branches were about 50 years old by my *kumu*'s estimation.) I got happy for a while when the leaders announced that they wanted to share all the living plant bounty that decorated their stage. *Great*, I thought, *I can ask for those* hala pepe, *grow them and replant them in the forest*. I went down after the performance and greeted three men in the *hālau* that I know personally. I explained my quest to grow the ancient *hala pepe* branches, and waited patiently while they greeted family and friends and took pictures. My friend came back and told me, "Oh sorry, Heidi, they changed their mind. They're going to take all the Laka plants to the grave of their *hula kupuna* and burn them."

Auwē! How *pohō*! Is this the way to cherish and nurture our forests? People who love hula should be the first to cherish the plants in their growing, living state! Let's not let them become a *mele* of memory only.

LANDSCAPE USE: *Hala pepe* are gorgeous in the landscape, and their slow-growing nature is an attribute. Many people don't like big or fast-growing trees or the leaf fall and pruning involved. *Hala pepe* is a perfect, well-behaved tree that won't grow too big and doesn't shed leaves. Its shape and size can make a statement in the garden. It is also pretty and ornamental in a decorative pot.

PROPAGATION: Grow *hala pepe* from fresh, ripe seeds, with the pulp cleaned off. You can also grow it from tip cuttings and stems, but this is much less environmentally friendly. Please don't take cuttings from wild plants, only from ones thriving and robust in cultivation (in your own garden).

This is one that commercial growers should plant as mother plants in the nursery to take cuttings from or make air-layers, to get larger plants for the landscape industry. If mother plants were growing in the nursery or base yard, you could also collect the ripe seeds at the perfect time.

PESTS: Rats and pigs eat *hala pepe* in the wild. Fires, development, and other threats make *hala pepe* rare. Watch them in your garden and prevent any insect invasion or pests that might attack your *hala pepe*.

KOKIA

SCIENTIFIC NAME: *Kokia drynarioides, K. kauaiensis, K. cookei*
FAMILY: Malvaceae (hibiscus family)

Many kinds of hibiscus grow in Hawai'i gardens—the precious, unique, and even fragrant native Hawaiian species, species from all over the world that have been carried here by people, and hybrids between the foreign and native Hawaiian species. Did you know there are even two genera (the genus is the larger plant category; the species is a subset), *Hibiscadelphus* and *Kokia*, that are endemic to Hawai'i and totally unique? *Hibiscadelphus* has the Hawaiian name *hau kuahiwi*.

Once there were many species of *Kokia* on all the islands. Today, sadly, there are only 3 species of *Kokia* still in existence. They are *K. kauaiensis* from Kaua'i, *K. drynarioides* from the island of Hawai'i, and *K. cookei* from Moloka'i. *K. cookei* is the rarest. It is extinct in the wild.

Kokia have red or orange hibiscus-like flowers that are somewhat curved and tubular. Scientists tell us that these are highly evolved hibiscus relatives, designed for being fed upon and thus pollinated by the once abundant native Hawaiian birds. Birds see red very well, and the more nectar a plant can provide the more attractive it is to a bird. *Kokia* provide a beautiful and fulfilling *lū'au* for Hawaiian birds!

The flowers develop into woody seed pods with several large, rusty red–colored fuzzy seeds. The pods are very attractive and durable. The leaves are pointy, lobed, and light green, often with red highlights. The branches and trunk of *Kokia* are very soft and vulnerable.

It is thanks to botanical gardens and dedicated horticulturists that this plant is alive today. Waimea Arboretum is the garden that saved this plant from extinction—from toppling over into the abyss of *make*, die dead, no moa: extinct.

This is just one small reason why botanical gardens are so vital. Many species that would have become extinct in the wild are kept alive today through the horticultural diligence of botanical gardens like Waimea. While people are busy earning a living and raising and educating their *keiki* and doing all the other daily things, our forests and native flora and fauna are in deep trouble. Waimea Arboretum takes extraordinary steps to perpetuate these plants for our future generations and for the health and well-being of all Hawaiian species.

Plant lovers knew that *Kokia* were in trouble. The Moloka'i species was down to one plant in the yard of George Cooke. Waimea Arboretum plant experts took seeds and cuttings from the one lonely plant and tried all kinds of ways to grow this rare and wonderful Hawaiian plant. The seeds wouldn't grow and neither did the cuttings.

A bud of Kokia drynarioides *at the Amy Greenwell Botanical Garden in Kona* mauka. *The buds, flowers, and dry fruit capsules of this endemic genus are striking and unique.*

A super-rare kokia cookei, *grafted by Waimea Arboretum, growing at the Koko Crater Botanical Garden. It is sheltered and protected by many other rare dryland Hawaiian plants.*

Peneku Kaʻae wears a lei *of* Kokia *blossoms. Photo by Jean Cote.*

Seed pods of hau kuahiwi, *growing in the gulch at Wahiawā Botanical garden. Several fuzzy brown, easy-to-grow seeds are found in each seed capsule. You can also see some of the flowers that have been pollinated.*

Then they tried an old technique that takes a bit of expertise: grafting. That finally worked and they got a couple of *Kokia cookei* growing on the rootstocks of the other more vigorous *Kokia* species. Then tragedy struck! A fire burned down the Cooke home on Molokaʻi, and the last *Kokia cookei* tree burned up too! *Auwē!*

Fortunately the grafted *Kokia cookei* still was thriving at Waimea Arboretum and Botanical Garden (now Waimea Valley Audubon Center). They have shared plants with other gardens. Director David Orr and dedicated plant propagators like Erin Purple and Frani Okamoto (all volunteers at that point) continued to care for the *Kokia* and myriad other rare plants and tried to figure out how to grow more.

Tissue culture, micro propagation, and in vitro culture all look like promising tools for the propagation and perpetuation of *Kokia* and other rare plants from Hawaiʻi and around the world.

PROPAGATION: It is best to grow *Kokia* from seeds, if you can find viable seeds. This rare and vulnerable plant can also be grafted onto a stronger rootstock. *K. drynarioides* seems to be the strongest and most vigorous of the remaining *Kokia* species that are alive today.

LANDSCAPE USE: *Kokia* is very attractive and interesting in the landscape. One of the best places to see it well grown and displayed is at the Amy Greenwell Botanic Garden in Kona *mauka*. The *Kokia drynarioides* is simply grown, set in a lawn, and surrounded by a nice mulch dish of red cinders. The cinders are very beneficial to the *Kokia* and also protect it from damage by lawnmowers and line trimmers. The red cinders highlight the reds in the leaves and the bright red flowers. The woody seed pods also have a reddish cast.

PESTS: Many of the common garden insect pests can attack *Kokia* if it is under stress. Try to keep it in good health, well watered, and underfertilized. The soft wood is very vulnerable. Protect *Kokia* from slugs and keep mowers and line trimmers well away. Do your best, as with all natives, to prevent "Shindaiwa burn."

HAU KUAHIWI

SCIENTIFIC NAME: *Hibiscadelphus distans, H. hualalaiensis, H. woodii*
FAMILY: Malvaceae

Endemic

Hau kuahiwi is another endemic genus in the hibiscus family. It has silvery leaves, and its blossoms are even more curved and tubular than those of *kokia*. You can really see how they would be a perfect match for the curved beaks of Hawaiian honeycreepers like *ʻiʻiwi*. *Hau kuahiwi* can be a shrub (see page 49) or—with time and the right growing conditions—a small tree.

LANDSCAPE USE: Grow *hau kuahiwi* as a specimen tree or shrub.

You can grow it in a decorative pot. Try *hau kuahiwi* in a *hapa-haole* garden to make it harder for pests to zero in on. The silvery leaves and unique flowers are an asset in garden design.

PESTS: As with all natives, especially the hibiscus family, fertilize not at all or as little as possible. Lush, well-fed, nitrogen-rich plants attract and are vulnerable to many insects and other plant pests. If you "must do something," top dress with red or black cinders. They are attractive and beneficial and keep slugs away.

OTHER USES: *Hau kuahiwi* would make the most amazing lei if you could cultivate enough flowers. It also might attract native nectar-feeding birds to your garden, especially if you have a lot of native plants they love, like *'ōhi'a lehua*, *koki'o*, *māmaki*, and *koa*.

MĀMANE, MĀMANI

SCIENTIFIC NAME: *Sophora chrysophylla*
FAMILY: Fabaceae (bean family)

Endemic

Māmane is an attractive small- to medium-sized tree. It grows better in cool upland *mauka* gardens in areas like Wahiawā on O'ahu, Pukalani on Maui, or Waimea and Volcano on the island of Hawai'i.

It has pinnate leaves, silvery on the underside, and bright yellow pea-blossom flowers. These are followed by woody winged seed pods that are also attractive on the tree.

Māmane is an important tree in the forest. It composes classic subalpine *māmane-naio* forests found on Maui and the Big Island. These forests on the Big Island are home to the *palila*, a unique Hawaiian bird with a parrotlike bill. We Hawaiian naturalists like to recall the time when a little golden yellow Hawaiian bird with a big beak "went to Congress" to get laws passed to keep alien mouflon sheep off the mountain and out of the forests, which they were devouring and destroying. Mouflon like to munch on *māmane* trees, eating leaves and bark and the seed pods that are a vital food for the *palila*. Their sharp hooves also cut open the roots of *māmane* and compact the soil around the trees. This damage affects the trees, birds, and even native Hawaiian insects. Several species of Hawaiian picture-wing flies feed on and breed in the habitats provided by healthy *māmane* forests.

LANDSCAPE USE: *Māmane* is a great tree for upland gardens. It is very pretty and cheerful with its golden yellow blossoms and silvery leaves. The seed pods are handsome, and the bark becomes deep and furrowed and gorgeous with age and time.

PROPAGATION: Grow *māmane* from seeds. Older seeds may have to be scarified to enhance germination. The seeds are roundish, hard, and golden yellow.

Māmane growing at the base of a pu'u *at Haleakalā. Sustained measures to control and eradicate feral goats, sheep, cattle, and pigs have greatly helped nurture the* māmane *forests and native birds at Haleakalā.*

Close-up of the lovely blossoms of māmane, *prefect for a lei or as a food source and prime habitat for rare Hawaiian birds like the* palila.

Nāʻū from Lānaʻi blooming and growing in one of the Honolulu Botanical Gardens. The fragrance of this rare gardenia is unique and lovely. Horticulture has helped save this rare species that was once common enough for lei making with pili *grass.*

Nāʻū in Waiʻanae, in an area protected by the state's Division of Forestry and Wildlife. Note the metal rat band to protect the seeds. The tall, fire-loving, alien guinea grass from Africa needs to be controlled to save the nāʻū *from wildfires. The* nāʻū *could also use some companion plantings and more* nāʻū *for cross-pollination.*

NĀʻŪ, NĀNŪ

SCIENTIFIC NAME: *Gardenia brighamii*
FAMILY: Rubiaceae (gardenia family)

Endemic

Nāʻū is a native Hawaiian gardenia. It was once common in low dryland forests of Hawaiʻi. Precontact *moʻolelo* tell of the wondrous lei, sometimes braided with *pili* grass as a backing, that were made of *nāʻū* and given for special occasions, such as Hiʻiaka's visits to Molokaʻi and Oʻahu in her quest to bring Lōhiau to Pele.

Today there are fewer than 30 *nāʻū* trees in the wild. Happily it grows fairly well in gardens. Horticulturists, botanical gardens, and private gardeners and hobbyists who care about native plants have helped to save and perpetuate *nāʻū* and other rare Hawaiian plants.

Nāʻū is a single-petaled gardenia that looks something like a *tiare*, or Tahitian gardenia. The fragrance of *nāʻū* is distinctive. If pollinated, the flower develops into a seed pod with many, many seeds tightly packed inside and surrounded by thin orange fruit flesh. This may have been a food for Hawaiian birds.

PROPAGATION: The best way to grow *nāʻū* is from seeds. Collect ripe pods and break them open. Rinse in warm water and separate the seeds from the orange fruit pulp. Soak the seeds for 24 hours, and then sow them in a clean pot with sterile potting soil.

Nāʻū can also be grown from cuttings and air-layers. Now that there are many plants in cultivation, this is more feasible. Plants in cultivation often root better from cuttings than trees in the wild do. We may be able to graft *nāʻū* onto other species of gardenia to make the most of available propagation material.

LANDSCAPE USE: *Nāʻū* is a very handsome shrub or small tree in the landscape. You can trim and shape it as desired and use the cuttings to grow more *nāʻū* plants. As the plant matures, the bark gets more strikingly white, and this is a nice feature to utilize in the landscape. Plant it against a dark background and the glossy leaves and white flowers along with the bold white trunk will really stand out.

PESTS: Aphids and scale are sometimes a problem, as they can be with any gardenia. Try to plant *nāʻū* in full sun and provide well-drained soil. Use a light hand with nitrogen and use liquid soap and mechanical methods to control sucking insects and their accompanying honeydew and sooty mold.

MUNROIDENDRON

SCIENTIFIC NAME: *Munroidendron racemosum*
FAMILY: Araliaceae (panax and ginseng families)

Endemic

Munroidendron is a rare Hawaiian tree. There is only one species in the genus and it is endemic to Hawai'i. It has large leaves with silvery undersides and a unique flower structure called a raceme, with many small yellow flowers adorning the long, silver flowering spike that hangs down.

George Munro (1866–1963) was a cattle rancher and also an inspired Hawaiian naturalist who was passionate and scientific about Hawaiian birds and plants. Munro contributed greatly to the fields of ornithology, botany, horticulture, and conservation and did much to save and perpetuate Hawaiian birds and the forests they live in. Munro and his *paniolo* planted Norfolk pines on Lāna'ihale to catch fog drip and increase rain for the low island. They eliminated all feral pigs on Läna'i and fenced the best dryland forests at Kānepu'u to protect them from the cattle. Many plants and animals are still with us today thanks to the efforts and vision of Munro and his staff.

The whole genus is endemic to Hawai'i. Munro found *Munroidendron racemosum* growing happily in the lowlands at Mana, Kaua'i. Today it is found rarely in the wild, and never at such low, denuded elevations as Mana. It is found naturally in only three small areas on Kaua'i.

Munroidendron racemosum growing at the Honolulu Zoo in the nēnē *exhibit. The foliage is architecturally arranged, with handsome leaves that are silver on the undersides.*

PROPAGATION: Grow *Munroidendron* from seeds. Fruits will develop from pollinated flowers. They are berrylike, with many small, flat seeds inside. The ripe pulp is purplish. Separate the seeds from the pulp by soaking them in warm water and gently squishing them and swirling so that the pulp floats away, leaving the seeds. Fertile seeds germinate readily. Transplant into successively larger pots and then into the ground or into a large decorative pot.

LANDSCAPE USE: This is a very pretty medium-sized tree for the garden. The large, bold leaves are striking. They are silvery on the undersides—perfect for your moonlit garden. It is a neat tree to look up at from below—the leaves are so strikingly silver and boldly patterned. The flowers are silvery, with pale yellow petals, and hang down ornamentally. Plant it in partial shade and well-drained soil at low elevations and in full sun if you live higher up the mountain (at about 1,000 feet). *Munroidendron* needs well-drained soil to thrive. It also makes a very attractive and unique potted or container specimen plant. It may be possible to acclimatize it to grow in shade or inside. This is yet more creative horticulture that we should test out on this fabulous native tree.

Fruits of Munroidendron racemosum, *freshly harvested from the grove at Wahiawā Botanical Garden. Many flat seeds are packed inside each fruit head, and freshly cleaned, ripe seeds grow readily. The long raceme of silvery furred fruits is an attractive part of the tree.*

PESTS: Borers sometimes attack the somewhat soft trunks of *Munroidendron.* Try to keep plants healthy and free of any mechanical damage, especially to the trunk. Make a "mulch dish" with a black cinder top-dressing to ensure that mowers and line trimmers keep well away, and to highlight the whites and silvers of the trunk and foliage.

Cluster of kou *blossoms. The flowers of this native Hawaiian and Polynesian canoe-carried tree make one of the most gorgeous and easily made lei. The* lei *is light and easy to wear and also dries nicely.*

Lei kou, *worn by Lehualani Pau'iliha, of Moloka'i. Photo by Jean Cote.*

KOU, SMOOTH-LEAFED *KOU*

SCIENTIFIC NAME: *Cordia subcordata*
FAMILY: Cordiaceae

Indigenous

For years it was believed that *kou* was carried here purposely by the ancient Hawaiians and was thus a "canoe" plant. Recent fossil evidence, found by archeologists in coralline sinkholes on Kaua'i, shows that it is a native Hawaiian plant—it got here on its own. (Because *kou* is valuable for woodworking and for making medicines, dyes, and leis, the Hawaiians carried *kou* seeds here as well, on their great voyaging canoes.)

Kou is a perfect shade tree for leeward coastal areas like Waikīkī and Lahaina. It can grow in pure sand and drink salt water, but it does better with fertile soil and fresh water. It was a favored shade tree in the villages of old Hawai'i. To me, it has very refreshing shade. Its large, green, slightly drooping leaves form a fairly dense, rounded canopy. The leaves make great animal food and excellent mulch. The flowers drop on their own and are easy to string without a metal lei needle. This was a favorite orange-colored lei in old Hawai'i.

LANDSCAPE USE: *Kou* is an ideal tree for lowland leeward and coastal areas. You also see it growing fairly happily in more upland areas like Maunaloa on Moloka'i. It is a less thirsty tree and doesn't mind brackish water. It is not a very salt wind–tolerant tree though. We tried planting one in Lanikai, set back from the beach and protected by a *hau* hedge, but every new set of leaves that emerged was "burned off" by strong, salty trade winds.

Kou is a very pretty, small- to medium-sized tree that is gorgeous in parks, larger home gardens, or business landscapes (e.g., Beretania Street), and as a street tree. There are some very nice mature specimens of *kou* on Monsarrat Avenue in Kapahulu.

PESTS: A caterpillar that arrived in Hawai'i in the 1850s was devastating to *kou* trees and wiped out many of the mature ones. This explains the rarity of big, old majestic *kou* trees in Hawai'i. Some of the bigger, nicer ones are on the UH-Mānoa campus, at 'Iolani Palace (one of my favorites to visit when I'm in downtown Honolulu and in need of shade), and in Kamānele Park in Mānoa.

Kou is very tough in gardens, parks, and urban landscapes. Do protect it from "Shindaiwa burn" by keeping mowers and line trimmers well away from the trunks of *kou* trees.

OTHER USES: *Kou* wood is soft when freshly cut and easily carved, even without the use of metal tools. This is one reason it was so prized in old Hawai'i. The wood also has lovely patterns, grains, and colors and dries into a valuable hardwood. It was favored for making cups, dishes, and calabashes.

Kou makes a delightful old-time lei. It is lightweight to wear and has no strong perfume (a must for some sensitive lei wearers).

Growing Native Hawaiian Plants

Because it is light orange, you might mistake it for an 'ilima lei at a glance. This is a lei that we can easily envision the Hawaiians of old stringing without a metal lei needle. The flowers are collected after they fall from the tree and have a large *puka* perfect for stringing. *Hau* fiber, raffia, or *mai'a* all would make for fairly easy stringing. Try this for fun or with your *keiki* sometime.

PĀPALA

SCIENTIFIC NAME: *Charpentiera*
FAMILY: Amaranthaceae

Endemic

Pāpala is a soft-wooded tree or shrub. It can have green or waxy green paddle-shaped leaves, in an alternate arrangement on the branch, and the leaves often have a bright red or pink midrib. The flowering spikes are panicles about a foot long, with tiny flowers, which are also red. This combination of flowers and foliage is very attractive.

Steve Perlman, while nurseryman at the Lawai Garden at National Tropical Botanical Garden, gave me an extra seedling in 1977, which I planted in my parents' Makiki garden. It quietly thrives between a plumeria tree and a Fijian *pua kenikeni* tree. Truthfully, I gave it little care or attention, just watered it as I did everything else in the mini "urban forest."

We have given this pretty but tough plant away at many Arbor Day events held each November by volunteers on many of the islands.

Pāpala is also being grown in great quantities at the Limahuli Botanical Garden in Hā'ena on the north shore of Kaua'i. Massive forest restoration efforts are going on in Limahuli, and *pāpala* is one of the successful and thriving Hawaiian forest plants.

PROPAGATION: Grow *pāpala* from seeds or cuttings. The seeds are kind of small but are easy to collect and grow. Cuttings acquired from selective pruning can be propagated.

LANDSCAPE USE: *Pāpala* is a very pretty addition to a Hawaiian garden. Use this shrub or small tree as an accent plant or as part of a larger grove. The colors of the red-rib types give a bit of drama in shady or mostly green gardens.

OTHER USES: *Pāpala* is also known as the Hawaiian fireworks plant. The soft, light wood was collected and dried and stacked on high *pali* (cliffs). When there was a special occasion, the branches were lit and tossed over the cliff. They would burn and lift and spin off sparks in the winds, creating the effect of fireworks to enrapt watchers below, who would gather on the sands or in canoes off-shore. The *pali* of Hā'ena was a famous place for this. The fireworks story appeals to our visual and historical senses, and *keiki* always seem to get a kick out of it.

Some pāpala *have very ornamental coloration. Horticulturists select and cultivate good-looking plants like this and grow more for all of us to enjoy in our gardens.*

Pāpala *displaying an attractive burgundy flower spike. This plant was grown at Ho'olawa Farms on Maui by fabulous nurserywoman Anna Palomino. Photo by Kim and Forrest Starr.*

PĀPALA KĒPAU

SCIENTIFIC NAME: *Pisonia* spp.
FAMILY: Nyctaginaceae (bougainvillea family)

There are several species of *pāpala kēpau* in Hawai'i, inhabiting different zones of the forest. Three are indigenous and two are endemic. Botanists believe that there were at least three different colonizations of *Pisonia* into Hawai'i.

In addition, the possibly ancestral species *Pisonia grandis* grows in several botanical gardens. It is called *puka* or *puatea*.

The sticky fruits of *pāpala kēpau* were used to catch birds for their feathers. These feathers were used to make the helmets, feather lei, and cloaks of the *ali'i* that you can see in museums like the Queen Emma Summer Palace, 'Iolani Palace, and the Bishop Museum.

The story we tell *keiki* is that the bird catcher would put the sticky *pāpala kēpau* fruits on the favorite perches of feathered birds. When a bird got stuck, the bird catcher would pluck out the prized feathers, clean the bird's feet off with *kukui* nut oil, and release the bird back to the forest to live and grow new feathers.

The reality is that it was cold and lonely up there in the rain forest, even for a skilled tradesman like a bird catcher. If he caught a bird he probably pulled out the feathers and then cooked and ate it, to supplement his protein-poor diet. This probably contributed to the decline of rarer Hawaiian forest birds.

The leaves of *pāpala kēpau* are bold and paddle shaped, and the flower clusters are small yet pretty, in shades of pink and green. The sticky fruits, though, are the most notable things about *pāpala kēpau*. They are like the tar baby—amazingly sticky and persistent. Collect some seeds in a plastic bag and you will need a lot of patience to extract them for planting.

The seeds are a fun, living lesson for *keiki*, showing how seeds might have hitchhiked on a bird's feathered body to get to Hawai'i. The seeds also trap a lot of insects (*keiki* find this cool yet gross), helping control pest insects in the garden.

LANDSCAPE USE: *Pāpala kēpau* makes a bold statement in a garden with its large, tropical-looking leaves. Species can be matched to the microclimate of your garden. Plant *pāpala kēpau* as a shady overstory for other plants or as an understory for taller trees.

Pāpala kēpau is also a plant with potential for use indoors. Some growers and gardeners are testing it in low-light, air-conditioned, and other challenging interior spaces.

PESTS: We don't know of many pests for *pāpala kēpau*. We need to grow this plant more and study all aspects of growing it and keeping it healthy and vigorous in the garden.

Pāpala kēpau *growing in a moist, protected gulch of the Honouliuli forest reserve in the Wai'anae Mountains. Note the sticky-headed fruits, poking out from the leaves, waiting to catch a passing insect.*

UHIUHI

SCIENTIFIC NAME: *Caesalpinia kauaiensis*
FAMILY: Fabaceae

Endemic

Uhiuhi is a rare tree of dryland forests. It was once much more common and reached larger sizes, as you can see from the black-and-white photos in Joseph "Pohaku" Rock's epic book *Native Trees of the Hawaiian Islands* (1931). *Uhiuhi* once were tall, majestic trees with valuable and useful hardwood.

So what happened? People arrived, bringing pests and changing the way the land was used. They burned and bulldozed and brought in "chompers and stompers" (hooved grazing animals like cattle, sheep, pigs, goats, and deer) on purpose and pest insects by mistake.

PESTS: Black and coffee twig borers are very destructive in *uhiuhi*. They are associated with fungus and the fungus galleries that nurture the baby twig borers inside the trunks of the tree. These weaken and can kill *uhiuhi* and other vulnerable native trees and plants.

Spraying the bark with Dursban, Merit, or other powerful systemic chemicals will protect them from borers. On the other hand, since poisonous chemicals are bad for us and the environment, perhaps it is better to leave the trees untreated. There is an old specimen *uhiuhi* at the botany courtyard garden at UH Mānoa. Many of us learned what *uhiuhi* is from this tree. It is riddled with borers yet has continued to flower and fruit over the years. Maybe all those inquiring, plant-loving minds and the hot air of stressed students seeking a shady and nurturing space have helped keep it alive.

OTHER USES: The rich, dark, hard wood of *uhiuhi* was used to make valuable war weapons, paddles, and other implements and tools like ʻōʻō (digging sticks). Visit the U.S. Army Museum, next to the Hale Koa Hotel, to see some of these classic wood weapons of war.

OLOPUA, NATIVE HAWAIIAN OLIVE

SCIENTIFIC NAME: *Nestegis sandwicensis*
FAMILY: Oleaceae

Endemic

Olopua is the most common Hawaiian tree in some forests. Along with *lama* it makes up the main species in the dryland forest at Kanepuʻu on Lānaʻi. It is also fairly common in other mesic and dryland forests.

Olopua has shiny green leaves with a pointed tip. Sometimes the midrib is pinkish. Small flowers are followed by green and then ripe blackish purple fruit.

Only a few botanical gardens and some private gardens grow *olopua*. It is not as easy to germinate or grow as it might look. The

Uhiuhi *flower head displayed amidst the feathery foliage. A red-brown seed capsule is visible in the lower left corner. New* uhiuhi *can be grown from the seeds in the pod. This plant is growing at the Amy Greenwell Botanical Garden in Kona.*

Lei uhiuhi. *Photo by Jean Cote.*

Olopua *blossoms in lush display after a nice wet Hawaiian winter.* Olopua *and* lama *are the main forest trees of the Kānepuʻu dryland forest on Lānaʻi, but few* olopua keiki *develop, even when the alien axis deer are kept out of the forest. If the flowers are pollinated and seeds develop fully, new* olopua *can be grown from seeds.*

pollinator or seed-dispersing insects and birds may be missing or very rare.

PROPAGATION: *Olopua* can be grown from seeds, although the germination is sometimes poor and often sporadic, with seedlings slowly coming up over several months.

It can probably be grown from cuttings or air-layers, and tissue culture of young seeds and immature embryos looks fairly promising. Greg Koob and now Nellie Sugii of Lyon Arboretum have been working on micropropagating this important Hawaiian tree.

Kanepuʻu has many healthy, good-looking trees, which during some years set abundant seeds that look as if they should grow. Rats like to eat them and so do wild turkeys. We bagged the trees to prevent predation. Many were collected and grown in nurseries on Lānaʻi and Oʻahu, but seed germination was fairly low. The seedlings grew slowly and often died inexplicably. Other techniques can and should be employed to grow more *olopua*.

PESTS: As noted, rats will happily eat *olopua* seeds, and they and mice sometimes chew on the bark for moisture if the weather is dry. Wild turkeys eat the fruit, but it may grow if it lands in a favorable spot. Axis deer from India and other grazing animals impact the trees by browsing on the leaves, rubbing the bark with their antlers, and stomping the roots.

Twig borers also attack *olopua* and weaken the trees with their internal feeding and fungus-spreading activities. Keeping the *olopua* as healthy and vigorous as possible and using preventative insecticides like systemic Merit may help combat the borers.

ABOUT THE AUTHOR

Heidi has played at propagating plants since small kid time. She began volunteering at Foster Botanical Garden when she was 17 and worked her way up from nursery aid to horticulturist and finally to director of all five Honolulu Botanical Gardens (Foster, Wahiawā, Koko Crater, Hoʻomaluhia and Liliʻuokalani). She was an apprentice gardener at National Tropical Botanical Garden, at Longwood Gardens, and the Royal Horticultural Society Gardens at Wisley, England, and holds a certificate in public administration and a master's degree in horticulture. She was education coordinator for the Hawaiʻi Plant Conservation Center of the National Tropical Botanical Garden and Oʻahu/Lānaʻi preserves manager for the Nature Conservancy of Hawaiʻi. Heidi is landscape director for the Hale Koa Hotel, writes a gardening column for the *Honolulu Advertiser*, and runs a horticultural consulting business that specializes in landscaping with native Hawaiian plants and xeriphytic landscapes. Her television feature "The Morning Garden" appears weekly on the early morning news on KITV, Channel 4.

Heidi and Beatrice Krauss, volunteering as Hawaiian lei plant identifiers at the Kapiʻolani Park Lei Day Contest and celebration, 1993. Note their lei poʻo of palapalai and ʻōhiʻa lehua. The black lei worn by the author is mānele, or Hawaiian soapberry, seeds, made by the Hui Hana volunteers of Lyon Arboretum.

The author stands next to one of her favorite cultivated koa trees, growing in the landscape in Lānaʻi City. Photo by Coleen Carroll, National Tropical Botanical Garden.